Caronia

Legacy of a 'Pretty Sister'

David F. Hutchings

SHIPPING BOOKS
PRESS

First published 2000 by Shipping Books Press
P.O. Box 30, Market Drayton, Shropshire TF9 3ZZ, UK
© David F. Hutchings, 2000

British Library Cataloguing in Publication Data
A catalogue record is available for this book from the British Library
ISBN: 1 900867 03 6 hardcover
ISBN 1 900867 04 4 paperback

Design and layout by MJP, Doveridge, Derbyshire
Printed and bound in the United Kingdom by Amadeus Press, Huddersfield, Yorkshire

Contents

Left: The first *Caronia* (1904–1932) is shown at her best in this postcard from a painting by Sam Brown. It was this ship, one of the 'Pretty Sisters' that would leave a legacy that would last for nearly a century.

Peter Newell Collection

Acknowledgements

Within the pages of such a small book about three magnificent ships it is only possible to include so much information. I have chosen to write about the ships themselves with a little about those who made them their livelihoods but very little about the passengers who, in the great majority, only knew the ship for the duration of their personal voyage or cruise.

I make no apology for concentrating most of these pages on the second *Caronia* – THE *Caronia* to many – as her fame as the 'Green Goddess' still evokes great passions in both ex-crew and passengers.

The third *Caronia* will only have been such for a short period by the time that this volume appears and I have therefore only briefly described her under her original name of *Vistafjord*.

To the many who willingly helped with invaluable information, photographs and encouragement – my sincere thanks and gratitude. If I have omitted a name from this generous group of people I apologise:

Bill Archibald; Peter Ashton; R. Aspinall; George Beck; Tammy Beltle; Frank Blake; Captain Ian Borland; Peter Boyd-Smith of 'Cobwebs' Ocean Liner Memorabilia, Southampton; Bob Brown; Bob Bruce-Grice; Mrs Sam Campbell; B. Cosens; Des Cox of Snowbow Productions; Arthur Crook; Basil Devenish-Meares; Captain Michael Dodds; John Eaton; Mr Edwards; Willie Farmer; Charles A. Haas; William Herzel; David Hicks; Alex Hutchings; Carola Ingall; Pamela Jackson; Captain Peter Jackson; Peter Jelly; the late Captain John Treasure Jones; Harry Jupe; Don Kent; Pat Lawless; Alison Lyndsay; Mick Lindsay; Iain MacKenzie; Michael MacLaverty; the late Commodore Geoffrey Marr; John Maxtone-Graham; Larysa Mitchell; John Moore; Peter Newell; Keith Newman; Sally Parsons; Jeffrey Sankey; Eric Sauder; Len and Margaret Thompson; Marcia Tubbs; Kenneth Vard; John Vaughan; David Williams ('Alby'); Captain G. D. Williams; Edwin Wilmshurst and Richard de Kerbrech, lifelong friend and advisor.

– and the following organisations:

Corporate Communications Department, Atlantic Mutual Companies, N.J.; Public Record Office, Kew; Imperial War Museum, Lambeth; National Maritime Museum, Greenwich; University of Liverpool (Special Collections and Archives); National Archives of Scotland, Edinburgh; National Museums and Galleries on Merseyside (Merseyside Maritime Museum); London Museum (Museum in Docklands); *Southampton Daily Echo*; *Liverpool Post & Daily Echo*; Southampton Central Library (Special Collections); Dock Museum, Barrow; Guildhall Library, London; Titanic International; Tyne & Wear Archives; The Ulster Folk & Transport Museum, Co. Down; Naval Historical Branch (MOD).

Sincerest thanks to Bill Miller for his generous Foreword, to Simon Fisher for his painting for the cover and my gratitude to Eric Flounders and Michael Gallagher of Cunard Line Limited for persuading me to change my original title of '*Mauretania and Caronia*' and expand it to the present one. At Shipping Books Press, thanks to Peter Johns and all for promptly and enthusiastically making the brave decision to publish at such short notice and to Linda Machin my appreciation for her patient and sympathetic editing of my manuscript and her choice of illustrations from the mass of material submitted. My thanks also to Alex – the younger of my two lovely daughters – for deciphering my manuscript and putting the text onto disk and to Sandy – my wife – for 'holding the fort' during the hectic weeks of writing.

Through various organisations I have attempted to trace the originators of many of the photographs that I have used to illustrate the work. Where I have been unsuccessful I have acknowledged sources where I can and I apologise for any unwitting infringements. Personal photographs from ex-crew members I have acknowledged but where I have no note of the originators other such illustrations are accredited to '*Caronia* Re-union.'

May the members of the latter long swing the lantern!

Dedication
To Pamela (née Jackson) and Peter Jackson
whose destinies the *Caronia* changed
and to
Alex

Foreword

What a marvellous trio of ships, each of them named *Caronia*! It is a name well known not only in British shipping circles, but worldwide. Like *Mauretania*, *Lusitania* and *Berengaria*, it has that certain flavour, that ring to it, that belong to the great Cunard Line ships. It somehow creates an image of a great passenger ship ploughing through the seas: strong and sturdy and dependable, but above all majestic. It was often said that the Cunard Company produced some of the best looking ships of all time. And indeed they did.

The first *Caronia* was a handsome twin-stacker, unpretentious and forth-right. Her all-white superstructure was balanced upon a long, sleek black hull and the twin stacks offset by a pair of towering masts. The lifeboats were nested, one upon the another, in the old Quadrant davit system. Markedly for her time, she had very few top-deck ventilators, especially when compared to the slightly newer near sisters *Lusitania* and *Mauretania*. Nearly thirty years later, when she went to the breakers, the *Caronia* of 1905 still looked quite well. There was an agelessness about her handsome exterior.

A now deceased friend, born in England but who often 'commuted' to New York in the 1930s, once missed a sailing from Southampton of the *Berengaria*. Cunard thought-fully re-routed he and his parents to Liverpool for the next day departure of the *Caronia*. It didn't seem to matter that the older ship would take nine days as opposed to the six of the *Berengaria*. But it all turned out to be a wonderful, most memorable experience, one that he often recalled in more recent times. The *Caronia* by then was an 'old gal,' as he called her. The innards were dark wooded, almost ponderous, very Edwardian. There was no running water in the cabin. Instead, it had to be fetched by a steward. The bathrooms were shared and the corridors narrow and cluttered with overhead piping. The ship moaned and creaked more than any other my friend had yet sailed in. Steady streams of black smoke poured out of the funnels. And except for reading, table games and Sunday church service in the lounge, there was, he recalled, little to do. Even for the 1930s, it was a look to the past, to that era of turn-of-the-century steamers. My friend returned to England on the maiden voyage of the *Washington*. What a contrast she must have been to that old Cunarder!

The second *Caronia*, the legendary 'Green Goddess,' launched just after the Second World War, was pure dreamboat. She was the first big luxury liner designed for full-time cruising. To me, she always seemed 'larger than life.' She had enormous proportions: a stout form, a huge single stack and a towering tripod mast atop the wheelhouse area. In fact, she was quite a modern-looking ship for her time and certainly contrasted to the likes of the three-funnelled, ventilator-topped *Queen Mary*, almost amazingly built little more than a decade before, or the low-decked, squat-stacked *Britannic* of 1930. Onboard, the *Caronia* was often said to be the most luxurious liner afloat, even more so than first class on the *Queen Mary* and *Queen Elizabeth*.

I saw the 'Green Goddess' very often at New York in the 1950s and 1960s. I remember one particularly frosty, but perfectly clear January afternoon. Every colour seemed richer than usual: the grey-green of the Hudson River and the sun's late day golden flashes in the windows of the Manhattan towers. Tugs, barges, ferries and a few of those railway carfloats shuttled about. Several freighters, the old breakbulk kind, filled the slips. But the real purpose of my braving the brisk winter wind was to await the four o'clock arrival of the *Caronia*. It was actually something of an event just to see her. She made only a half-dozen or so calls at New York each year. These were timed to her long cruise departures. But she was always one of my favourite ocean liners and on this occasion, as reported in the daily shipping schedules of the *New York Times*, the timing was just right for a schoolboy. She was due to dock at Pier 90 just after dark, at 5 o'clock. She was late, no doubt, due to

Above: The first *Caronia* on sea trials in 1905.
NMGM, Merseyside Maritime Museum

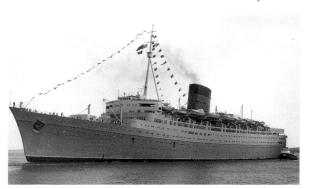

Below: The second *Caronia*, the 'Green Goddess,' dressed overall on a gala occasion.

Peter Boyd-Smith

Above: *Vistafjord* in an exotic location on one of her many cruises. *Cunard*

storms in the western Atlantic. She was also, rather unusually, inbound from the sunny Caribbean: coming north from Trinidad, Barbados, Kingston and Nassau. Having begun her voyage at Southampton, she had delivered British 'winter dodgers' to those sun-drenched islands before coming to New York to refuel and replenish, and then start her annual 95-or-so day cruise around the world. I was thrilled to finally see her appear in the lower Hudson. She was worth waiting for.

I also remember visits to the *Caronia* in her final days with Cunard, in 1966–67. In fact, I was aboard just prior to her final Cunard voyage, an autumn Mediterranean cruise. The date was October 1967 and, rather appropriately, it was a very foggy morning. Internally, the ship that once defined the ultimate in sea-going luxury seemed dated, dowdy, even worn in places. After all, she had been in service for nearly twenty years. Her interiors had become something akin to museum pieces. Art Deco and even later, lighter Deco was not yet in revivalist vogue. Consequently, this once very grand Cunarder looked of another age with her lino flooring and chintz-covered chairs, the leatherette sofas and the polished veneers. A new, brighter, often far flashier age was upon us – those white, wedding cake-style cruiseships. Momentarily, ships like the brand new *Oceanic*, *Sagafjord* and *Kungsholm* caught our attention. And within two years, a far different Cunarder, the *QE2*, would have her debut amidst an advertising campaign 'Ships have been boring long enough!'

I also recall a cold February day when I last saw the *Caronia*, but by then tarnished and neglected as the Greek-owned *Caribia*. The year was 1974 and the ship's days were clearly numbered. She was being pulled apart and her pieces price-tagged for auction. At her West 14th Street berth in Manhattan, enthusiasts and collectors and perhaps even a few former passengers walked ashore with cocktail tables and glass panels, china teapots and stainless pots. Even those big ivory-coloured phones caught the eyes of collectors. It was all quite sad. The age of ships like the former *Caronia* had passed and those who realised it wanted a keepsake.

The third *Caronia* is assuredly one of the most luxurious ships cruising today. She has a great warmth, a clubbiness, an embracing quality about her. She is noted for her fine service and food, and her select itineraries. Very much, she follows in the tradition of the second *Caronia*, another 'big yacht'. And she even looks similar with her dominant single stack placed amidships and the single mast atop the bridge. I have made several trips on her, but in her earlier days as the *Vistafjord*. One, an around-Britain cruise in July 1990, was timed to coincide with Cunard's 150th anniversary celebrations. I was a guest lecturer, talking about the great liners, past Cunarders mostly. We anchored off Spithead one misty morning and were quite close to the mighty *QE2*. Other ships were present and small craft huddled about us. Great excitement filled the air. Anxiously, most of us remained along the open decks. The actual celebration day was upon us. By midday, the royal yacht *Britannia* arrived, carrying the Queen and Prince Philip. Together, they reviewed this assembled fleet. Loud cheers went up as the royal couple sailed past. Flags were dipped, horns sounded and sirens screeched. On cue, a member of the Concorde fleet flew overhead. The *Vistafjord* later followed the *QE2* into Southampton to await the evening's fireworks display. It was a grand occasion for a great ship and her historic owners.

A book on the splendid ships called *Caronia* is long overdue. The selection of evocative text coupled with fine photographs should please ocean liner buffs and cruise travellers and even staff members, past and present alike. In these superb pages, the two earlier ships return to life while the third gloriously embarks on a new career. For one, I am most grateful to David Hutchings.

William H. Miller
Secaucus, New Jersey
Fall 1999

Below: *Vistafjord* and *QE2* met in Southampton before the Cunard 150th Anniversary review in the Solent in August 1990. Part of the finance needed to build the *QE2*, launched in 1967, was raised by the sale of the then-ageing 'Green Goddess.' *David Hutchings*

INTRODUCTION
'Ships with Names Like Jewels'
(Joseph Conrad)

Nineteen ninety nine – an important year for the Cunard Line. Within the span of this, the last year of the last decade of the last century of the millennium many memorable events have taken place. Within Cunard – one of the oldest shipping companies in the world – the major event of the year must have been the acquisition of the Line itself by Carnival Cruises who, besides operating its own line of 'fun-ships,' has acquired and revitalised with new ships other older and much respected, overseas shipping companies. Their future plans for Cunard bode well for a brilliant future with one – and possibly two – new ships being planned for the North Atlantic service under the banner of 'Project Queen Mary'.

1999 marked the thirtieth anniversary of the maiden voyage of the ever popular *Queen Elizabeth* 2, an occasion celebrated by a special, on-board lunch. The year also marked the fiftieth anniversary of the maiden voyage of one of the Cunard's most famous ships – the legendary *Caronia*. The second Cunard vessel to have borne this name, she was more popularly known by devoted crew members and passengers alike as the 'Green Goddess'. Although thirty years have passed since the 'Green Goddess' made her exit from the Cunard fleet her reputation as the epitome of luxury cruising during the 1950s and early 1960s still lives on and her memory still evokes strong passions in those who served in her.

At the end of the year another vessel will assume the illustrious name of *Caronia* – Cunard's *Vistafjord*, already established with a reputation as a comfortable ship of great beauty.

The first of the three Cunarders to be called *Caronia* was built in 1905 and was one of an experimental pair of steamships. She and her sister-ship, the *Carmania*, were almost identical except for one important difference – their engines. These two elegant Edwardian vessels were rightly called the 'Pretty Sisters' and gave many years of comfortable service to their owners and faithful years of war service to their country.

Indeed, all three *Caronia*s have each been a part of a popular and most attractive pair, even though the latter two *Caronia*s were separated in their building from their respective sisters by several years and, in the case of the 'Green Goddess' by a war.

So the 'new' *Caronia* is warmly welcomed and will, it is certain, soon earn her own epithet, thereby joining an élite club of well-loved ships. Her already achieved reputation as a ship of great beauty and popularity assuredly qualifies her to become another of the great *Caronia*s thus maintaining the 'Legacy of a Pretty Sister'

David F. Hutchings
Lee-on-The Solent, Hampshire
October, 1999

Left: A wonderful photograph of the second Caronia, the legendary 'Green Goddess,' taken as she picks up speed after leaving New York.

Cunard/ Willie Farmer Collection

CARONIA (I)
The 'Pretty Sister'
1904–1932

1
'Brilliant and Unauthorised'

Sunday 4 August 1889 was a special day. The new White Star Liner *Teutonic* had arrived in the waters of Spithead and The Solent between the Isle of Wight and the English mainland to be shown off to some special guests. In the afternoon, interrupting their sailing at Cowes, Edward Prince of Wales, his nephew Kaiser Wilhelm II Emperor of Germany and Prince Henry of Prussia came on board to inspect the vessel.

Of special interest were reinforced steel plates concealed under areas of decking which could be removed for guns to be bolted into position thus converting the liner into an Armed Merchant Cruiser. This idea re-introduced a practical concept from centuries before when merchantmen armed with cannon were taken up from trade to be used as warships.

The German Emperor was impressed. 'We must have some of these', he said to an aide, and a further incentive was added to what developed into a race for naval supremacy between Great Britain and Germany.

Eight years later in 1897, Saturday 26 June dawned another special day. In celebration of Queen Victoria's Diamond Jubilee a vast fleet had assembled at Spithead. Not only were warships of the mighty Royal Navy lined up with representatives from foreign navies, but the Prince of Wales was again present with his royal German nephew.

Teutonic was again present as the royal party on board the Royal Yacht *Victoria and Albert* (led by the Trinity House Yacht *Irene* and followed by other ships in grand procession) sailed through the scores of warships that were lined up in four rows.

One of the ships in the procession that followed the Royal Yacht was the 12,950 gross tons Cunard liner *Campania* of 1892 which, along with her sister-ship *Lucania*, had held the Blue Ribband for the fastest crossings of the Atlantic.

On completion of the royal progress and whilst the visiting dignitaries and naval staffs were still on their various vessels, a small, sleek private yacht burst into view with flames belching from her funnel and a turbulent white wake following her path. Speeding through the lines of assembled warships the interloper reached unheard-of speeds of 40 knots.

The 'brilliant and unauthorised' guest was the *Turbinia*. Built and owned by the Honourable Charles Parsons the vessel was driven by his own invention, the turbine.

The display revolutionised naval thinking and, by February 1905, the Royal Navy had planned their *Dreadnought*, which would render obsolete through its armament and propulsion all other warships in the world.

The turbine was also being adopted elsewhere. The Scottish coastal steamer *King Edward* of 1901 was the first large ship to incorporate the engine. The Allan Line brought out their Atlantic steamships *Virginian* and *Victorian* in 1904 and the other big shipping companies were also taking notice.

In 1902 the British White Star Line was taken under the financial umbrella of J. Pierpoint Morgan's American combine, International Mercantile Marine, which then proceeded to finance the British company, ultimately leading to the building of the *Olympic*, *Titanic* and *Britannic*.

The British Government was fearful that the White Star Line's ships would be denied them in time of war as Armed Merchant Cruisers and were just as fearful that the Cunard Line might also be swallowed up in Morgan's American empire. The Government decided to loan Cunard the finance to build two giant vessels that could be converted into cruisers in times of crisis. The two ships would reflect two lessons learned over the previous decade – those of the armoured cruiser capability and the

turbine. These ships would become the *Mauretania* and *Lusitania* both launched in 1906 and of just under 32,000 gross tons.

But before these two giants could be built Cunard needed experience of the turbine. John Brown's Shipyard on the Clyde had received a contract from Cunard to build two sister ships and, at their suggestion, the design of one was altered to incorporate turbine engines as the main power plant whilst the other sister would retain the more familiar quadruple expansion reciprocating engines.

These two vessels would become the *Carmania* and her sister-ship – the *Caronia*.

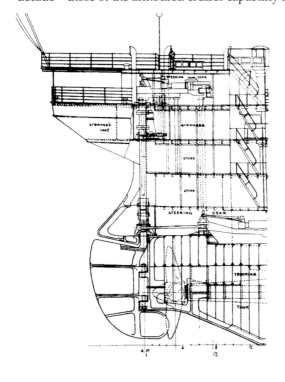

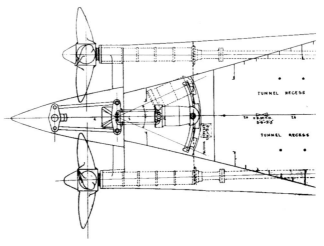

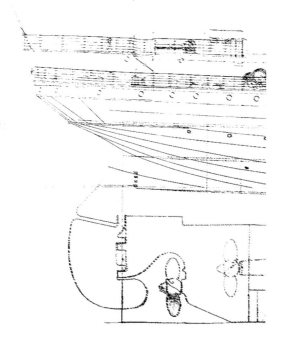

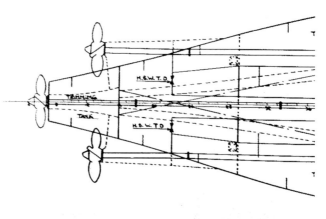

Caronia and *Carmania* were built as a pair of experimental ships to give Cunard experience of new turbine engines before putting them into larger vessels. These engineering drawings show the differences in the under-water stern design and propeller arrangement between the *Caronia* **(above left and right)** and *Carmania* **(below left and right)**. *Caronia* was fitted with the usual twin screw quadruple expansion reciprocating engines while *Carmania* was adapted to take the new turbine engines to drive her triple screws.

Drawings courtesy of NMGM (Merseyside Maritime Museum)

2
One of a Pair

Contracts for the two sisters were placed in 1903. Because of the turbines, the *Carmania* was given three propellers (in lieu of *Caronia*'s two) which necessitated a re-design of the structure around the propellers and rudder. As a consequence, *Carmania* was completed eight months behind her sister. The keel of the *Caronia* was laid down on 21 September 1903.

With the disappearance of sails as a necessary appendage in case of engine failure or loss of propeller and the substitution of steel for iron, the sisters sat higher in the water than any previous ship. Two tall, well-spaced funnels and masts with enough rake to be almost dashing, along with an elegant sheer, earned the two liners the epithet of the 'Pretty Sisters'.

The ships were 678 feet overall in length, had a beam of 72.2 feet and a draught of 32 feet forward and aft. At 19,687 gross tons the *Caronia* was slightly larger than her sister. At the time of her launch this made her – until the advent of the *Mauretania* and *Lusitania* – the largest of the Cunard fleet and the largest ship to have been launched from a British mainland shipyard.

In her construction her inner keel was 50 inches wide and 1 inch thick, the vertical keel 36 inches wide and between 20 and 15 twentieths thick (steel thickness were specified in twentieths of an inch) and the outer was 50 inches wide but of a similar thickness to the vertical.

Frames were spaced 2 foot 9 inches apart, reducing to 2 foot 6 inches fore and aft, and were 10 twentieths of an inch thick. The first row of steel plates next to the keel (the 'A', or garboard, strake) was 52 inches wide and 20 to 15 twentieths in thickness and the other strakes were thinner at 18 to 13 twentieths.

Floors (the vertical plating) making up the cellular double bottom were 14 twentieths at keel to 12 twentieths at the turn of bilge. The superstructure was 7 twentieths thick and covered a length of around 500 feet. Her foredeck was 120 feet long and the after-deck 50.

Beams that supported decks were made from channel bar of 9 x 3½ x 3½ inches, reducing in size in the superstructure. Deck plating was mostly 8 to 7 twentieths and support pillars in between decks varied in diameter from 2 inches high up in the structure to 5½ inches in the Engine Room.

Steel rivets were used throughout the shell plating; Upper and Bridge Deck stringers; on strakes next to hatch openings on the Upper Deck; Shelter Deck stringers and plating throughout and all machined rivets throughout the structure. Remaining rivets were of best iron.

Caronia, Yard No. 362, was launched on 13 July 1904 by Mrs J. H. Choate, wife of the Ambassador of the United

Right: With vertical floor plates of the double bottom in place the structure is now ready to receive the tank top plates of the inner bottom and to support the lower ends of the frames. Smoke from a rivetter's furnace curls into the air as the first thousands of 1.5 million rivets are applied. *National Archives of Scotland*

Above: This cutaway diagram of *Caronia* by J. J. Jelly was presented with *The Boy's Own Paper*.   *David Hutchings Collection*

States. After her launch, *Caronia* was fitted with her engines, boilers and all the trappings that went to make a luxury Atlantic liner as well as an emigrant carrier.

Both sisters had the same boiler layout with which to produce their engine-powering steam. In the stokehold there were three single- and four double-ended boilers in the forward boiler rooms and two single and four double in the after. These worked at 210 p.s.i. and the three furnaces at each end of the boilers had a total of 52,139 square feet of heating surface. The furnaces were fed from 5,000 tons of coal stored in bunkers forward, between and aft of the stokeholds.

On the *Caronia* the steam produced was fed into two quadruple expansion reciprocating engines, the four cylinders being 39, 54½, 77 and 110 inches in diameter. The 20,000 i.h.p. produced gave a service speed of around 18½ knots through two four-bladed propellers placed just forward of a balanced rudder.

Four anchors were carried. One bower anchor of the stockless type weighing 170 cwt and the other 150 cwt. A stream anchor (excluding stock) was 42½ cwt and the kedging anchor 23 cwt.

500 fathoms each of stud and stream chain cable was of 3⅜ and 1⅞ inches respectively. 130 fathoms of 7 inch circumference steel-wire towline was included along with 440 fathoms of steel hawser ranging from 5½ to 3¾ inches in circumference. Manilla hawsers of 6, 8 and 10 inches circumference totalled 880 fathoms.

There were nine decks; Boat; Promenade; Bridge; Shelter; Upper; Main; Lower; Orlop (i.e. decks froward and aft of the Engine Room) and the Engine Room (or tank tops). Engine seats were 1 inch thick. Practically all decks were planked with pitch pine, which was left as bare wood in Third Class and Steerage areas.

Classed at Lloyds 100 A1 to their 'Three Deck Rule', she had a registered length of 650 feet and she was 52 feet deep from keel to Shelter Deck and 72.2 feet wide.

There was accommodation for around 3,592 passengers divided into 800 First (or Saloon); 320 Second (or Second Cabin); 1,458 Third and 1,014 Steerage Class.

Beneath the **Bridge,** which housed the Chart Room and Wheelhouse, the nine decks were arranged as follows: Officer's quarters were on the **Boat Deck** as was the Lounge (the *Caronia* was the first liner to use this term) aft of the forward funnel uptakes and the Marconi Room aft of this. Sixteen lifeboats were carried in accordance with the Board of Trade regulations for a ship of 10,000 gross tons or more.

The **Promenade Deck** housed deluxe en-suite rooms right forward and a First Class entrance was aft of these. A Writing Room; First Class Drawing Room and Smoke Room completed the public rooms on this deck.

Other deluxe First Class staterooms occupied the forward areas on the **Bridge Deck** with 'ordinary' First Class accommodation aft of this and the Purser's Bureau lay just forward of an ornamental well that overlooked the First Class Dining Room on Shelter Deck below. The Second Class Drawing Room was further aft as was the Smoke Room for this class.

Sited forward of the Bridge front on the **Shelter Deck** was a Third Class entrance (through which the main mast passed) with a Third Class Smoke room and Second Class cabins aft. The First Class Dining Saloon occupied the area between the funnel uptakes, aft of which were further First Class staterooms and the Second Class Dining Room and bedrooms. Another Third Class entrance house completed the deck layout along with the steering gear compartment.

Bridge
1 Chart room
2 Wheelhouse
Boat Deck
3 Firemen's Retreat
4 Marconi room
5 Lounge
6 Officer's Quarters
7 Captain's Day-room or Cabin
Promenade Deck
8 First Class Smoke-room
9 Pantry to Smoke-room
10 First Class State-room
11 First Class State-room
12 Upper Promenade Deck
13 First Class Drawing-room
14 First Class Writing-room
15 First Class Entrance
16 Cabin de Luxe

Bridge Deck
17 Second-class Smoke-room
18 Second-class Drawing-room
19 First Class State-room
20 First Class State-room
21 Library
22 Ladies' Retiring-room
23 Passage-way
24 Purser's Bureau
25 First Class Entrance
26 Cabin de Luxe
27 Printer's Shop

Shelter Deck
28 Steering-gear Compartment
29 Third-class Entrance
30 Second-class Bedrooms
31 Second-class Dining-room
32 First Class State-room
33 First Class State-room
34 Music Room
35 First Class Dining-saloon
36 Entrance to First-class Dining
37 Second-class Bedrooms
38 Third-class Smoke-room
39 Third-class Entrance

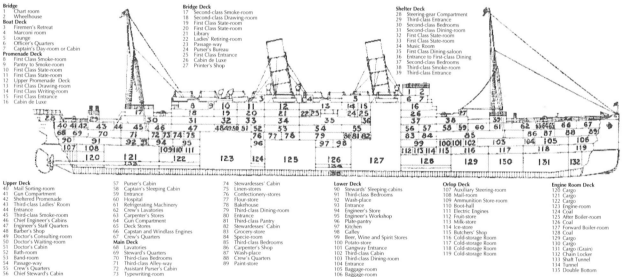

Upper Deck
40 Mail Sorting-room
41 Gun Compartment
42 Sheltered Promenade
43 Third-class Ladies' Room
44 Entrance
45 Third-class Smoke-room
46 Chief Engineer's Cabins
47 Engineer's Staff Quarters
48 Barber's Shop
49 Doctor's Consulting-room
50 Doctor's Waiting-room
51 Doctor's Cabin
52 Bath-room
53 Band-room
54 Passage-way
55 Crew's Quarters
56 Chief Steward's Cabin

57 Purser's Cabin
58 Captain's Sleeping Cabin
59 Entrance
60 Hospital
61 Refrigerating Machinery
62 Crew's Lavatories
63 Carpenter's Stores
64 Gun Compartment
65 Deck Stores
66 Capstan and Windlass Engines
67 Crew's Quarters
Main Deck
68 Lavatories
69 Steward's Quarters
70 Third-class Bedrooms
71 Third-class Alley-way
72 Assistant Purser's Cabin
73 Typewriting-room

74 Stewardesses' Cabin
75 Linen-stores
76 Confectionery-stores
77 Flour-store
78 Bakehouse
79 Third-class Dining-room
80 Entrance
81 Third-class Pantry
82 Stewardesses' Cabin
83 Grocery-store
84 Specie-room
85 Third-class Bedrooms
86 Carpenter's Shop
87 Wash-place
88 Crew's Quarters
89 Paint-store

Lower Deck
90 Stewards' Sleeping-cabins
91 Third-class Bedrooms
92 Wash-place
93 Entrance
94 Engineer's Store
95 Engineer's Workshop
96 Plate-pantry
97 Kitchen
98 Galley
99 Beer, Wine and Spirit Stores
100 Potato-store
101 Gangway Entrance
102 Third-class Cabin
103 Third-class Dining-room
104 Entrance
105 Baggage-room
106 Baggage-room

Orlop Deck
107 Auxiliary Steering-room
108 Mail-room
109 Ammunition Store-room
110 Boot-hall
111 Electric Engines
112 Fruit-store
113 Milk-store
114 Ice-store
115 Butchers' Shop
116 Cold-storage Room
117 Cold-storage Room
118 Cold-storage Room
119 Cold-storage Room

Engine Room Deck
120 Cargo
121 Cargo
122 Cargo
123 Engine-room
124 Coal
125 After Boiler-room
126 Coal
127 Forward Boiler-room
128 Coal
129 Cargo
130 Coal
131 Cargo (Grain)
132 Chain Locker
133 Shaft Tunnel
134 Tunnel
135 Double Bottom

Upper Deck had much of the accommodation for senior crew including Chief Engineer, Purser, Chief Steward and the Captain's sleeping cabin. The Hospital, other medical facilities and Doctor's Cabin were here too.

Main Deck was mainly given to Third Class accommodation and Dining Saloon with some crew quarters and stores.

On the **Lower Deck** forward were large dormitories for Steerage passengers, mostly emigrants travelling to the United States on a one-way ticket along with all their belongings, customs, habits and beliefs. Various stores not only separated the forward from the after Steerage accommodation but probably separated the single men from families and single girls!

Stores were mainly on the **Orlop Deck**, with those forward being insulated. On the **Tank Tops** below were chain lockers; three forward and one amidships cargo holds; coal bunkers forward and aft; forward and aft stoke holds; Engine Room; No. 5 Hold (with fresh water tanks on each side). No. 6 Hold with shaft tunnels port and starboard and the lower steering gear flat. The cargo holds were served by four hatches, two forward and two aft, placed fore and aft of the masts.

The ship's double bottom, 5 foot deep, contained water ballast; reserve feed water; and trimming tanks fore and aft. The *Caronia* had twelve main transverse bulkheads and was the first Cunard ship to have the watertight doors in the bulkheads hydraulically operated from the Bridge rendering, so the publicity brochure said, the ship practically unsinkable.

As 1904 drew to a close the *Caronia* drew near to her departure from the Clyde.

Above: Ready for launching. Sliding ways have been built and the after poppet supporting the stern has been erected. The last of the blocks on which the *Caronia* had been built have yet to be removed. The complex arrangement of the construction of the stern clearly shows, as do the propellers. Note the practice of bolting propeller blades to the boss, an arrangement which led to many ships losing a blade in service.			*National Archives of Scotland*

Below: 13 July 1904, ten months after keel laying. The moment of launch when a ships meets its element. The deceptively simple, elegant lines of an early Edwardian steamship can be seen to full advantage. Two vertical pipes on the foredeck are the shafts for two tall ventilator cowls. This was a feature that the 'Pretty Sisters' had in common for only a short while, as those on the *Caronia* were removed shortly after her entry into service.			*National Archives of Scotland*

3

Luxury for All

The décor of the interiors of the *Caronia* were finished according to class, with greatest attention, as usual, being given to the First – or Saloon – Class staterooms and public rooms.

The First Class Dining Room extended centrally through two decks, the central gallery being surrounded by an ornate carved screen finished in white with gold details. The room contained tables that were typical of the day. Long tables seated 46 people and others had room for 5, 8, 16 or 11. Swivel chairs with arms were chained to the patterned lino-covered deck and potted plants adorned the tabletops. Beneath the dome was a central round table but away from the centre, tables were square or oblong. Carpet runners were laid in the walkways.

The Saloon (First) Lounge again had a lino-covered deck with large oblong carpets of oriental design placed where required. Large, ribbon- and square-checked upholstered armchairs and pouffés and heavy tables with wooden armchairs provided the furnishing.

Floral tapestry upholstery, side settles, square tables and wood framed padded armchairs graced the Saloon Drawing Room and a fireplace was sited at one end.

A grand piano was the main feature of the Music Room and a glazed dome overlooked round tables with armchairs. Glazed sideboards, curtained portholes and intimate side alcoves presented a pleasing appearance.

The Writing Room, perhaps designed with ladies in mind, had a lighter Regency feel to it. Shaded lights, slender columns, striped upholstery, writing tables and bobbled curtains gave the room a cosy – but airy – appearance.

The Verandah café had not reached the heights of perfection that a similar room would a few years later. The deckhead was painted white, with rivet heads not yet concealed beneath plasterwork. The underside of structural beams were darkly painted to give the appearance of 'old oak' beams in a country house. Bulkheads and partitions were again white enamelled with an artificial, heavy-looking, half-timbered finish. Ivy was trained up these walls as well as around the columns. Carpet runners in walkways, cane or wickerwork furniture were well lit by large, glazed windows.

The First Class staterooms were also decorated in the style that lay between Chintzy Victorian and Golden Age Edwardian. Wallpaper, lots of mahogany, plastered ceilings, bunks and ladders or brass-bound bedsteads, heavily patterned eiderdowns and plump pillows (most of the beds with side panels to prevent unwanted exits during rough weather!), settees, stained-glass sash windows complete with railway-style leather straps, heavily figured ventilation ducts, bare light bulbs and trailing flexes – all made up the décor that passengers would find in their various grades of stateroom.

Second – or Second Cabin – Class was less exciting. Their Dining Room had long tables along which were placed swivel chairs with heavy round bases.

Above: A deeply buttoned mattress is indicative of a First Class stateroom. The curtained sofa could berth a juvenile. The curtains not only ensured privacy but also provided easy insulation as central heating was not too effective! A mahogany encased wash-station plus water decanters would be appreciated by a discerning traveller. The quality of the finish to the the ship can be seen in the French polishing on the chest of drawers.
National Archives of Scotland

Right: The First Class Lounge of *Caronia*, the first room afloat to be designated as such.
Cunard / Charles A. Haas Collection

Above: First Class Dining Room.
Cunard / Charles A. Haas Collection

Top left: The First Class Smoking Room – a gentlemens' club afloat. *Cunard / Charles A. Haas Collection*

Middle left: A Second Class Smoke Room, refinements over Third (*see bottom right*) included a skylight, upholstered seats and carpet runners. The pitch pine deck is still reminiscent of a village hall or urban town hall used for social occasions. Bare electric bulbs represent the norm.

National Archives of Scotland

Bottom left: The Third Class Smoke Room may look austere but the panelling, especially, would make it luxurious for many travellers who were not used to such refinements. Electric lights and wood flooring were also luxuries not experienced in many of the homes being left behind. The Smoke Room looked over the foredeck so its male occupants could see the New World approaching after nine days at sea.

National Archives of Scotland

Right: Third Class Dining Room.   *Cunard/*
                                      Charles A. Haas Collection

Below: A Third Class cabin. Bare decks; a single wash unit for the four inhabitants to use during the nine-day crossing; one gimbaled light and painted planked bulkheads and ship's structure contrast sharply with decor in First Class. The eiderdowns of First Class are here replaced by thin cotton bedspreads patterned with the Cunard lion to prevent pilferage.
                    Courtesy of University of Liverpool Library

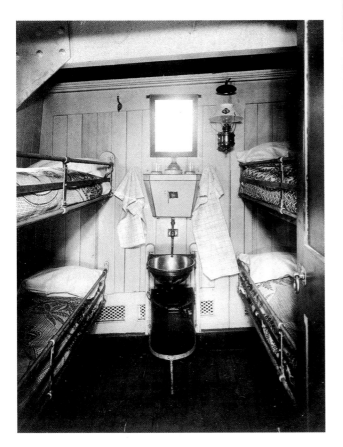

Aspidistras in pots and exposed deck planking under the tables completed the décor. The Drawing Room in this class had button upholstered settees and canework chairs. Relief patterned plasterwork between beams provided the decorated ceiling and a small bookcase provided the source of some leisure.

The Ladies' Room was similar to the Drawing Room but had lighter-looking furniture but the Smoke Room reflected its use as a gentlemen's club. A bare wooden deck, carpet runners in walkways, dark panelling and upholstered settees and settles, square leaded windows and a small, mirror-backed table and cupboard gave an impression of functionality.

Second Class Cabins contained four berths (curtained for privacy and warmth, as in First Class) and double washstands were provided with swivel sinks that emptied into containers.

Although Third Class was basic, for many of its passengers the conditions on board were probably more than many had dreamt of. To many, it was luxury to have

running water, inside toilets that flushed, wooden floors, electric lighting, regular meals and even stewards to wait at table.

The Third Class Dining Room was sparsely furnished. Bare, scrubbed, wooden decks; un-upholstered, wooden swivel chairs; long tables that had solid 'fiddleys' fixed transversely in between each seating position as well as around the tables' edges; large china water jugs and bowls; single sets of knife, fork and spoon; and bare, painted pillars and deckheads. What appeared to be an oil-cloth covered the tables, barely reaching to the edges.

Third Class fared about the same in their Smoke Room. Wooden Chairs, settees and settles; bare decking; very few bare lights, but at least there were portholes. The Sitting Room was similarly sparse.

Two, three and four berth cabins in Third had a single, galvanised washstand (shared); a lack of privacy curtains around the bunks which were supplied with thin-looking eiderdowns and blankets.

Steerage were berthed in five large dormitories sleeping 296, 178, 84, 178 and 250, and some of this space could be partitioned off to create additional Third Class cabins if necessary. Lavatories were communal. Here decks were laid with black and white checked rubber tiles; there were marbled shelves with washbasins, above which was one large mirror. In the men's toilets there were three marbled urinals. Marbled cubicles had louvered wooden doors.

The accommodation on these lower decks was kept basic to provide cheap fares. It also allowed for easy cleaning and, if necessary, fumigation.

By the end of 1904 the *Caronia* was complete. Painted in the striking colours of the Cunard Line she truly looked magnificent. Her two tall, elliptical funnels looked especially splendid in their red and black colour scheme which, by giving the funnels two instead of three thin black bands, looked very elegant indeed. Her black hull had been painted up to the Bridge Deck and this would provide the original external distinguishing difference between herself and her sister *Carmania*.

4
Early Years and Icebergs

At the end of January 1905, the *Caronia* left the shipyard of John Brown and Co. at Clydebank and sailed down the Clyde to Greenock and then on to Liverpool where she was dry-docked to have her bottom plates and propellers cleaned of growth that had accumulated during her time alongside the fitting-out jetty. The remains of the launch gear was also removed. Painted and pristine she returned to Greenock in readiness for her trials.

Trials were run on 4 February along the Skelmorlie mile and she achieved 19.62 knots.

Returning to Liverpool to store, the *Caronia* sailed under the command of Captain R. C. Warr on her maiden voyage on the 25th. Sailing via Queenstown (now Cobh) in Ireland, she reached New York nine days later.

Sailing from New York on 16 May the *Caronia* encountered fog and her captain had to take action to avoid a sailing vessel and a German liner. As a result the *Caronia* grounded off South West Spit near Sandy Hook. She was reported as 'resting easy' and no danger was seen as there was little sea running.

Assistance was sent in the form of tugs and it was expected that she would refloat herself on the early morning tide. This did not happen and the tugs put lines aboard. After much manoeuvring, the liner's stern was freed but her bows remained firmly embedded.

The evening tide was 'unusually high' but the Cunarder refused to move. It was decided that, if she did not float on the next morning's tide, some of the cargo in her forward holds would be trans-shipped into lighters.

By the late afternoon it was reported that the ship had been refloated at both ends but was still held at a position under the Bridge where there was only 28 feet of water. Anchors were laid out on each quarter for the ship to kedge herself off with the assistance of the tugs but, still luckily undamaged, this did not happen.

After lightening the ship, the *Caronia* was at last freed on the third day with the aid of seven tugs. She returned to New York, stopping at the Narrows to check for damage, anchoring at Gravesend Bay. She resumed her interrupted voyage to Liverpool on the afternoon tide.

She remained on the North Atlantic route until

Top: Captain R. C. Warr commanded *Caronia* on her maiden voyage from Liverpool to New York on 25 February 1905.
Peter Newell collection

Left: Smoke bellows from the *Caronia*'s funnels during her full speed trials in January 1905. Her name is just distinguishable at the bow. The ship would be in a light condition for her speed trials (minimal coal, water, stores, etc) as can be seen from her riding high in the water.
National Archives of Scotland

October when she transferred to the Mediterranean emigrant route (at the same time giving First Class passengers a sunshine cruise). Her ports of call now included Fiume, Palermo, Trieste, Genoa, Naples, Alexandria, Gibraltar before going back to New York.

In November 1905, the *Caronia* experienced a fire in her electric fan room at 1.00 am after the ship had passed Brow Head, whilst homeward bound. The fire was extinguished before the vessel reached Queenstown and the short-lived excitement amongst the passengers died down almost as quickly as the flames. The damage was very slight.

She returned to the North Atlantic in April 1906, remaining on that route until June 1907 when she made a single cruise to Gibraltar and Cadiz. Later in the year, she made a November cruise to Madeira, Gibraltar, Naples and Fiume before returning to New York.

Her yearly pattern was now set, North Atlantic in the Summer and Autumn, the Mediterranean for cruising and to pick up emigrants in the Winter and early Spring.

Whilst anchoring at Fiume on March 4 1908, the *Caronia* parted her cable and she swung around, striking and damaging the *City of Khios*.

Above: *Caronia* Captain Barr, captain at the time of the *Titanic* disaster.
Peter Newell collection

In late March of 1912, she returned to Liverpool from a cruise that had taken her to Madeira, Gibraltar, Algiers, Monaco and Naples. The summer runs from Liverpool to New York resumed and, as usual, her two wireless operators, Robert Leith and W. E. Hutchinson, were kept busy. The two men were employed to operate the on-board service mainly to make money for the Marconi company. Passengers' messages made the profits but the wireless operators also sent messages for the ship, telegraphing her position to shore stations and sending and receiving official messages for the Bridge.

Sailing from New York on her return journey on 11 April the liner's wireless room began to receive, transmit, relay or just listen in to messages for the largest liner in the world then making her maiden voyage – the White Star Line's *Titanic*.

On 14 April both ships were in favourable positions to allow exchanges of radio messages. Hours previously the *Caronia* had passed through an enormous icefield drifting down from the north and had also passed several icebergs. The *Caronia*'s Captain Barr sent an early morning message to the wireless room to inform Captain Smith of the *Titanic* of the dangers they had seen and had heard reported by other ships:

> 'Westbound steamers report bergs, growlers and field ice in 42N from 49-51West. Barr.'

Captain Smith on the *Titanic* took the message to his chart room and marked the chart before pinning the telegram on the notice board for the information of his officers on subsequent watches.

Four hours later *Titanic* responded:

> 'Captain *Caronia*. Thanks for message and information. Have had variable weather throughout. Smith'.

Another two hours passed by before *Caronia* relayed a message from *Titanic* to the Holland-America ship *Noordam* that had obviously sent a message of congratulations to the brand new liner:

> 'Captain *Noordam*. Many thanks. Had moderate variable weather throughout. Compliments. Smith.'

In the early evening as the distance between *Titanic* and *Caronia* increased a cryptic, perhaps personal, message was received on the latter vessel, relayed by the French Line's *La Provence*:

> 'Riggs, *Caronia*. Many thanks. Love to both. Smith.'

Again through *La Provence*:

> 'Captain Barr, *Caronia*. Greetings. Speddens.'

(Probably Mr Frederic Spedden, a First Class passenger on *Titanic*).

Titanic's wireless apparatus was very powerful and transmitted to *Caronia* for relay to the *Noordam*:

> 'Captain steamer *Noordam*. Thanks for message. Had fine weather, no fog. Bon Voyage. Reuchlin.'

Five hours later the beautiful *Titanic* struck an iceberg (11.40pm by *Titanic*'s clocks) and began to founder. Passengers were put off in lifeboats and the stricken liner sent out wireless messages for help. Many of these messages were intercepted and relayed during the course of the tragedy by the *Caronia*. She played her part during that night, although too far away to render any actual assistance.

At 12.30am (times are '*Titanic*' time') the *Caronia* informed the White Star liner *Baltic* of the accident that had happened to the latter's fleet mate:

> 'MGY (*Titanic*'s call sign) struck iceberg. Require immediate assistance.'

Twenty minutes later, to *Baltic* again:

> 'SOS' (the new distress call). 'MGY. CQD' (old call for assistance) 'in 41.46N, 51.14W. Wants immediate assistance.'

The *Baltic* responds and alters course. 01.15 *Baltic* to *Caronia*:

> 'Please tell *Titanic* we are making towards him.'

The *Caronia* manages to tell the sinking liner the news:

> '*Baltic* coming to your assistance.'

At 01.47 *Caronia* hears *Titanic* calling but her signals are too indistinct to understand. A few minutes later the Cunarder hears *Frankfurt* telling *Titanic* that she is over 150 miles away.

This message, like so many others received by the *Titanic* that night, was of little use. Thirty minutes later the giant liner up-ended and slid beneath the surface of a flat calm sea. Over fifteen hundred people died with the *Titanic* but the 705 people in lifeboats owed their survival to wireless telegraphy as well as to the Cunard liner *Carpathia* which rescued the survivors early in the morning of 15 April.

Caronia had played a part in the greatest maritime tragedy to date, arriving at Liverpool a few days later.

5

Tours of Duty

After the excitement of the previous April, the *Caronia* settled down to her yearly, seasonal routines. Captain Rostron, hero of the *Carpathia*, took the ship over briefly in December 1912. Other captains to have the *Caronia* as a command since her maiden voyage had been Barr, Le Brecht, Charles, Pentecost, Pritchard, Smith (C.A.) and Turner.

Cunard's naval architect, Leonard Peskett, read a paper before the Institution of Naval Architects on 3 April 1914, in which he spoke about the design of steamships from an owner's point of view. In it he compared the performances of the *Caronia* (fitted with reciprocating engines, twin screws, running at an average of 80 r.p.m.) with the *Carmania* (compound turbine engines, triple screws and 175 r.p.m.). He said 'The ships have now been on service for over eight years, and the results do not warrant the adoption of direct acting turbines to drive a ship of this type at a speed of 18 knots, the coal consumption for the *Carmania* being considerably greater than that of the *Caronia*.' The *Caronia* seemed to be the company's favourite.

The *Caronia* arrived from New York on 22 July 1914 and went into dock ready, it was thought, for a refit. But at 11am on 4 August 1914 when war was declared against Germany, for Great Britain and its Empire a way of life started to end.

Immediately, many liners which had been built to become Armed Merchant Cruisers were requisitioned into Government service.

A telegram dated 1 August 1914 had been received by Cunard's Managing Director. From the Director of Transports at the Admiralty, it confirmed a message of the day before and stated 'that circumstances of grave national import which will shortly be announced by Royal Proclamation render it necessary to requisition the

Left: Captain Pritchard.
Peter Newell collection

S.S. *Aquitania* and the S.S. *Caronia* for immediate use in Government Services as Armed Merchant Cruisers.'

The telegram also requested Cunard's co-operation in preparing the ships for sea and the company was reminded that they had agreed to provide coal, engine-room and deck stores for four months, along with utensils, bedding, etc.

Captain H. Shirley Litchfield, R.N. was appointed Captain of the *Caronia* with her usual civilian captain, Charles Smith, who had been in command through 1914, acting as Navigator. James 'Bill' Bissett who had been Fourth Officer on the *Caronia* in 1907, rejoined his old ship just before the War and would stay on as her First Officer. Bissett had been Second Officer on the *Carpathia* during the rescue of the *Titanic* survivors and later would become Commodore of the Cunard Line.

On 2 August, the *Caronia* was classified as a Class 'B' Merchant Cruiser and was allocated to Devonport for manning purposes. The Royal Proclamation was made on 3 August and the *Caronia* was officially requisitioned under Charter Party T.99.C.

Captain E. G. H. Gamble, R.N., was put in charge of preparing the *Caronia* and *Aquitania* for war and 5,000 men busied themselves stripping fittings and trappings of luxury from the two liners – enough to fill 2,000 wagons.

Captain Litchfield, a force to be reckoned with, sent the following telegram to the Admiralty:

'Insufficient engineers for the Engine Room. Service conditions require frequent alterations of speed, starting, stopping and reversing. It is customary in merchant service to double-bank engineers when manoeuvring engines. These conditions are frequent on present service and I consider request for four additional Engine Room Artificers RNR reasonable and submit four be detailed to join at Huskisson Dock, Liverpool not later than 9am Wednesday. If Artificers RNR not available propose engage four engineers from shore. Captain HMS *Caronia*'

The captain was informed that RNR engineers were not available and that he would have to exercise his second option. The Admiralty telegraphed Cunard in

Below: Although of the *Carmania*, her sister ship, these guns would have been similarly fitted to *Caronia* during the First World War.

From A Merchant Fleet at War *by Archibald Hurd*

Liverpool requesting that the company supply Captain Litchfield with the men he needed.

During the conversion woodwork was stripped out, armour plates fitted in vulnerable areas, eight old 4.7 inch, quick-firing guns were bolted onto the built-in pads, (four forward in pairs and four aft), and bulwarks were cut away to allow training of the guns. A six foot Barr and Stroud range finder was fitted. Sandbags and rope matting were located for extra protection and two of the ship's cargo holds were modified to become ammunition magazines, complete with means of flooding the magazines should there be a risk of explosion. Two searchlights and two semaphores were also fitted on her upper decks.

The ship was painted in black up to the Boat Deck with black funnels and within a week she was ready for war duties. The liner was commissioned as HMS *Caronia* on 8 August in the Huskisson Dock, Liverpool.

On Monday the 10th she sailed at 1pm on her first patrol. Outside the Mersey Bar her gun crews fired one broadside at a time to test the guns and then the ship proceeded South. She stopped early the next morning to rendezvous with some warships before carrying on.

The first ship that she stopped was the Leyland Line's *Nessian* which did not know that the war had started. She later stopped the *Ben Vrakie* and the *Maria da Larrinaga*.

By now she was a member of Force 'E', a squadron which comprised His Majesties Ships *Doris* (flagship), *Minerva*, *Isis*, *Venus* and *Juno*. Other AMCs in the squadron were *Mauretania*, *Aquitania* and *Lusitania*. (The appointments of *Mauretania* and *Lusitania* were later cancelled).

Over the next few days *Caronia*'s crew practiced war-routines with her ammunition supply parties competing against each other.

One evening her signal lamp failed and she was nearly fired on by the *Doris* who did not receive a reply to her demand for identification.

The first excitement came on 19 August when, in position of 49.40N, 11.53W, two sailing vessels were seen. One, a French schooner, was sent on her way but the other, was a large four-masted barque with her name painted out. *Caronia* raised a German ensign and when the barque raised hers in reply the Cunarder raised the White Ensign and ordered the German ship to heave to and lower sail.

Heaving to herself, the *Caronia* sent boats with an armed boarding party to the barque which turned out to be the *Odessa* of Hamburg of 3,040 tons gross. 102 days out of Chile, the *Odessa* had 4,850 tons of nitrate on board which could have been used for the manufacture of explosives. By 11.30pm the *Caronia* took the *Odessa* in tow and headed towards Berehaven in Ireland. The German captain, C. Gabler, had learned that his country was at war with France but had not heard about Great Britain's involvement. He treated his British 'guests' with hospitality whilst under tow. The next day the party arrived in Bantry Bay and the *Odessa* was officially handed over to the receiving customs authorities. The barque was officially condemned on 8 December, as was her cargo two weeks later, though she survived her sentence, reappearing after the war and sailing on for many more years under other names.

Above: A woven rope anti-splinter mat such as this on sister ship *Carmania*, would probably have been fitted to *Caronia*.

From A Merchant Fleet at War *by Archibald Hurd*

After refuelling in Liverpool the *Caronia* was off again. Two years previously she had been in contact with the Dutch steamer *Noordam* during the tense hours before the *Titanic* had sunk. Now, on 7 September, after a three hour chase, the Cunarder was firing shots across the Dutchman's bows as the ship had not stopped as requested. After sending over a boarding party and discovering 290 Germans and Austrians on board, the *Noordam* was taken under escort until later handed over to HMS *Doris* to convoy her to Queenstown.

By mid-September the *Caronia* was stationed at Halifax, Nova Scotia and on patrol around the Ambrose light vessel in case any of the big German liners laid up in New York attempted to make a run.

A Danish steamer, the *United States*, was stopped and boarded by a boat from *Caronia* and Germans on board were taken prisoner, later being transferred to a British vessel by the boats from HMS *Niobe*.

On 13 October the *Caronia* was *en route* to Halifax at full speed to coal when she was recalled to take over a war prize on the 14th from HMS *Suffolk*. This was the German registered tanker *Brindilla* and *Caronia* towed her to Halifax at 6 knots.

It was in September that news came through of her sister ship's gallant battle in the South Atlantic. HMS *Carmania*, also converted into an AMC, had disguised herself as the German Merchant ship *Cap Trafalgar,* and had then made contact with this very ship. By coincidence the Germans had cut off one of the three funnels of their ship and re-painted her to look like the *Carmania*!

The British liner had caught the German vessel coaling off the Brazilian island of Trinidad and in the ensuing fight, the only battle to take place between two AMCs, the *Cap Trafalgar* was sunk. As she sank the British cheered the gallantry of their German opponent.

For *Caronia* the next few months were spent on routine patrol off the Ambrose light vessel, returning

Above: The devastation on the Bridge of the *Carmania* after her battle with the *Cap Trafalgar*

Shipbuilding and Shipping Record

occasionally to Halifax to take on coal. Vessels were stopped – the *Caronia* sometimes firing a blank round to make her message clear – and searched. During her periods of patrol *Caronia* was accompanied at various times by HM ships *Glory*, *Suffolk*, *Niobe* and *Essex*.

Twice during the last months of 1914 the *Caronia* became flagship of the squadron as its admiral and his staff boarded for several days as a time. She would also collect mails from the warships and, along with her own, deliver the post to vessels *en route* to England.

Caronia remained in Halifax from late November (after a full month at sea) until early January as urgent repairs were required on serious boiler defects. These repairs took six weeks, after which she coaled and prepared for sea, sailing on 10 January 1915.

On 18 January she anchored in shallow water but lost her starboard anchor and 45 fathoms of chain.

31 January found her again in Halifax where she was due to pick up a relief crew of stokers arriving on the *Corsican*. Cunard men signed on for periods of six months at a time and the original stokers on *Caronia* had not pleased Captain Litchfield. He took exception to their unkempt appearance and it took some time for his staff to instill naval discipline and pride in appearance into the hard-working men.

The *Caronia* arrived at the base port in freezing conditions and Lieutenant Commander E. C. Roden wrote in his diary 'The ship was a wonderful sight – snow and ice from stem to stern; the sprays as they had come on board froze solid. Am in my new cabin, which is not above freezing – water bottle burst with ice. Spent a miserable night trying to keep warm'. The weather remained cold with fog and drizzle whilst the ship coaled but, when at sea again, the weather cleared.

She returned to Halifax on 22 March and during an 'Abandon Ship' exercise a fireman fell 38 feet from 'B' Deck into a boat and died from his injuries the next morning.

Five days later, she was back into freezing weather at sea. On Easter Sunday *Caronia* trans-shipped the squadron's mail to the *Lusitania* which had reverted to civilian passenger work after Winston Churchill had called her and the *Mauretania* 'Live Bait' following the successive sinking of three cruisers by one submarine in a few hours. The *Mauretania* was by now laid up in Liverpool awaiting a decision on her future.

A collision occurred at 9pm on 13 April when a large six-masted American coastal schooner, the 3,000 ton *Edward B Winslow* of Portland, Maine, collided with the *Caronia*, hitting her portside, abreast of her aft funnel. Both vessels received damage, the *Caronia* sustaining damaged bulwarks and a wrecked lifeboat and davits.

Next, to Halifax for coal, then on patrol in heavy snow. Two days later the temperature reached 90°F! Two more days fog, heavy rain, thunder and lightning.

On 1 May, a bright day with a slight mist, the *Lusitania* once again stopped as she was heading for Liverpool and the *Caronia* sent over the mails for home. On the 7th the ship heard that the 'Lucy' had been torpedoed and sunk off the Old Head of Kinsale with a heavy loss of life – including Americans. The resultant outcry would help those who wanted the United States to enter the war on the British side.

The next day the *Caronia* left Halifax yet again but this time headed toward Liverpool for a refit. She arrived, to the surprise of people in Liverpool, at the Sandon Dock on 15 May.

After a period in dry-dock from 9 June which included replacement of her old 4.7 inch guns with new 6 inch weapons, the *Caronia* sailed on 3 July. Shortly after departure she used her new guns to fire at what was thought to be a submarine. This tour of duty took the liner to Bermuda, then it was back to the New York patrol. Very little happened during this period – a fire in No. 2 Hold on 26 September and another in the Engine Room in the middle of January 1916.

In November some of the younger crew members, probably bored with the continuous patrols, applied to be sent to France where they thought they would see more action. Their applications were denied as, it was said, they served their King and Country just as much where they were.

A change in scenery in February when the *Caronia* moved to Chesapeake Bay. A collision with the steamer *Sergipe* in early March provided the only excitement of her last months as a patrol ship.

On 22 July 1916 she left Halifax for the last time on patrol and arrived in Liverpool on the 31st. On 7 August, just over two years since she was commissioned, the *Caronia* was paid off.

6

An Argument Over Sixpence

Caronia lay in dock in Liverpool in October 1916 gutted in readiness for her next service. The Admiralty pointed out that only sufficient work for her next purpose should be carried out and none done to refit her for any other use. In August it had been suggested by the Director of Transports that Caronia and Laconia be converted into cargo carriers due to 'a shortage of labour and a demand for cargo ships'. Nothing came of the proposal.

On 21 October, Trafalgar Day 1916, Caronia sailed to Halifax as a troop transport bringing to Liverpool 4,500 members of the Canadian Expeditionary Force. She was hired under Charter Agreement T.99.C at eighteen shillings and sixpence per ton for the two months she was used. As a troop carrier she came under the umbrella of the Principle Naval Transport Officer.

The Admiralty tried to enforce a reduction in long-term rates, paying Cunard in a lump sum only seventeen shillings per ton under a scheme to include her trooping duties as well. Cunard was entitled to receive seventeen shillings and sixpence per ton for Caronia's previous patrol work and objected to the Admiralty's attempt to obtain a reduction of sixpence per ton. The full sum was eventually paid after the case went to arbitration under Mr Butler Aspinall.

Returning to Liverpool Caronia later steamed down to Devonport where she remained, presumably undergoing overhaul and another conversion. On 5 January 1917, she sailed for Sierra Leone, Cape Town and Durban where she arrived on 17 February.

This tour would take South African troops from Cape Town and British troops from Bombay to Dar-es-Salaam as part of an Expeditionary Force into what had been German East Africa.

Above left: Caronia sails from Durban during the Great War packed with troops.
From A Merchant Fleet at War *by Archibald Hurd*

Above right: The "Comet" produced by soldiers on board His Majesty's Transport Caronia serving in the Indian Ocean. *Courtesy of University of Liverpool Library*

During one of the early transport voyages a group of soldiers organised a news-sheet called The "Comet". Printed on a foolscap sheet, folded in half, and priced at one penny, it lasted for twelve issues (including a 'Special Pictorial Number' which consisted of well-drawn cartoons) from 15 January to 2 March 1917. The "Comet" offered four pages of shipboard gossip, jokes, reports on shipboard activities, cartoons and hints on what to expect at various ports in the way of local customs, etc. To avoid a breach of security the ship's name was not mentioned anywhere in the publication. One of the humourous articles was a series entitled 'Things We Want to Know (by the Owl)' such as 'How the "Made in Germany" pencils for sale in the canteen came on board a troopship!'

A Sports Day held on 24 February was also marked by a specially printed programme, again without mentioning the ship's name. However Commander Diggle was mentioned as were several of the regiments on board, the latter breach of security necessary to identify the participants in the sports such as 'Bolster Bar' (for officers as well as NCOs and Privates); 'Sack Race'; 'Wheelbarrow Race,' etc.

Left: Painted in submarine-confusing dazzle paint, the *Caronia* was used to transport U.S. and Canadian troops across the North Atlantic from 1918. *Tom Rayner/David L. Williams Collection*

The *Caronia* was now stationed in the Indian Ocean as Expeditionary Force Transport No. G.1628. Her ports of call would generally be Durban, Bombay, Kilwa Kissiwiana, (140 miles south of Dar-es-Salaam) and Colombo with occasional calls at Dar-es-Salaam. A fire was discovered in No. 2 port coal bunker on 20 May and an explosion occurred on the 24th in the liner's No. 3 port bunker. One trimmer was injured, three received extensive burns and eight men were gassed. It took three days for the resultant fire to be extinguished in the bunker. The injured were transferred to HMS *Barjora* in Tunghi Bay as she was *en route* for Dar-es-Salaam where the injured men could be taken to hospital.

In 1917 she was painted in 'dazzle', a scheme of bold stripes and squares in black, white, blue and green. This scheme was designed by noted marine artist Norman Wilkinson, and its purpose was to break up the perspective of a ship and give a false sense of its direction when seen through a periscope. At the end of December the *Caronia* left Durban for Cape Town, Sierra Leone and New York where she became an Expeditionary Force transport for American troops.

In 1918 a deadly epidemic of influenza ('The Spanish Flu') was sweeping the world and, at its end, over twenty million people had died, their resistance reduced by the ravages and deprivations of war. The *Caronia* was not to escape. During one dreadful period between 5 October and 14 October nearly one hundred soldiers died on board of the bronchial pneumonia that followed the influenza. Some died within minutes of each other and most were buried at sea but some were interred when the liner called into Brest. Very few crew members succumbed to the disease.

The Great War shuddered to a halt a month after these on-board tragedies had occurred.

The influenza did not disappear however. In the early months of 1919 the *Caronia* was engaged on the Liverpool–New York run with occasional calls at Brest. Sixteen year old Steward's Boy Thomas Bell was sent ashore to St. Vincent's Hospital in New York in February suffering from pneumonia.

Captain C. A. Smith (*Caronia*'s Navigator on the Ambrose patrol) and her Captain in 1914 at the outbreak of war retook command around this time from Captain E. G. Diggle who had commanded the ship for much of the liner's tour as a troopship.

From March until June the New York call was augmented with a call into Halifax transporting Canadian troops.

The ship's boilers by this time must have been in dire need of an overhaul as twice during April blow-backs occurred, both events resulted in injuries. One fireman, G. Dullaghan, suffered burns to both hands and another J. Gallagher, suffered second-degree burns from a blow-back whilst cleaning a fire.

It would appear that the liner was handed back to her owners in June 1919 and she continued on variations of the Liverpool–Brest–Halifax–New York route until August.

She was repainted in Cunard colours, but her condition inside must have been dreadfully spartan. Only a few First Class cabins and the Smoking Room were available as these had been retained during the War as officers' accommodation and Wardroom.

In late August the *Caronia* returned from New York and called first at Plymouth, then Dover and on 12 September arrived for the first time at Tilbury on the Thames.

The *Caronia* did not return to London as planned at the end of November 1919 and it was thought that the proposed new service between London and New York had come to an abrupt end, possibly because of a 'chilly welcome of an autocratic port authority'! In reality the London docks were too busy and too crowded to take another liner because, due to American labour troubles, both the *Caronia* and *Saxonia* had reached London at more or less the same time. It was stated that the situation for large passenger liners would be eased in London once the Albert Docks were completed in mid-1920. Congestion for the time being was extremely bad and was exacerbated by the lack of rolling stock and barges.

Calls at le Havre, Southampton, Halifax and New York finished in Liverpool as 1920 began its second day.

For a week Liverpool was almost congested as London. The liner would remain here for over four

Above: Pretty Sister *Caronia* entering Tilbury Docks on 12 September 1919. The London call would then be postponed for a short while due to congestion in the great port.
Museum in Docklands (Museum of London)

months while she underwent a thorough reconditioning. Many of her pre-war fittings that had been kept in storage were renovated and replaced as her restoration progressed. New furniture and carpets were also installed.

Evidently, Cunard had earlier made an offer to the Government to have the *Caronia* and *Saxonia* refitted at Devonport, the Plymouth dockyard. But, because of the large amount of work in hand in the dockyard and a shortage of skilled labour, the offer was declined. Five months later, however, when the liner's refit was almost complete, questions were asked by Viscountess Astor in the House of Parliament as to whether the decision could be reversed as there were, by May, large numbers of unemployed men in Plymouth. Apparently, the Admiralty had offered Portsmouth Dockyard some time after refusing Cunard the use of Plymouth but, by then, the company had made other arrangements in placing their contract in Liverpool.

Trials had taken place on the *Aquitania* of the recently introduced Sperry gyro-compass and Cunard were pleased with the results. The compasses would be fitted in future on all new-buildings but they were also installed on the *Caronia* and *Carmania* during their post-war refits.

Cunard had already fixed the *Caronia*'s post-war

itinerary and this would include calls at Hamburg (P&O, British India and other British steamship lines had already re-started using this port) and the Queenstown call was resumed.

Caronia finally left the Mersey on Saturday 8 May 1920 fully booked with 2,000 passengers in all classes, proving that she had not lost her pre-war popularity. She made her first call at Queenstown for more than five years.

In September the *Caronia* returned to London and continued to use the port for the rest of the year sailing to New York as planned, using a combination of Plymouth, Halifax, Dover, Cherbourg and Southampton as ports of call *en route*.

On the last day of 1920 she left New York on her first post-war cruise calling at Madeira, Gibraltar, Algiers, Monaco, Naples, Alexandria, Shaleron Bay, Naples, Palermo, then back across the Atlantic to Boston, returning to New York nine weeks after her departure. The American tourists on board were under the joint guidance of American Express and Thomas Cook and Son.

Whilst at Shaleron Bay on 14 February 1921 one of three stowaways (found on 12 February) were put ashore into police custody. She was a 17 year old Greek girl, Christantina Gyplakides. Two British boys, John Noble (18) and William Johns (19), had also been discovered.

Left: Alexandria in Egypt was the easternmost port of call on the *Caronia*'s Mediterranean cruises. From here Thomas Cook arranged excursions up the Nile to Cairo, the Pyramids and the Temples at Luxor. 4 February 1921.
Shipbuilding & Shipping Record

Below: Captain E. C. Diggle (*right*) the long-serving master of the *Caronia*, and Staff Captain R. L. Alexander pose for the camera on the liner's Bridge during the 1921 Mediterranean cruise.
Shipbuilding & Shipping Record

Presumably, they were taken back to Britain. The *Caronia* seemed to be popular with younger stowaways as, in May that year, when the liner was once again on the North Atlantic ferry run, a 17 year old Spaniard, J. Grarira Ballara, stowed away in New York.

Just before one o'clock on the morning of 25 September 1921, the *Caronia* collided with a small sand sloop, the *John Anton*, which quickly sank. In the dark hours of the early morning the liner lowered her emergency boat and searched for survivors in the vicinity. Some small craft assisted in the search but, unhappily, none were found.

The *Caronia* stayed on the North Atlantic ferry run to Liverpool until three more Mediterranean cruises were undertaken back-to-back from New York, the first starting on 22 October and continuing through until 30 March 1922.

From March to November 1922 the *Caronia* sailed New York to Southampton via either Hamburg (where, on 15 August, a rope fouled a propeller) or Cuxhaven, Plymouth; Boston; Cherbourg then Liverpool–Queenstown–New York until February 1923.

It was in December of 1922 that Cunard, perhaps tempted by the profits to be made, decided to replace the Marconi wireless operators on their ships with their own men. A specially designed uniform was produced and a Senior Wireless Operator was given a rank equivalent to a Second Officer on the Bridge.

By now the *Berengaria* (ex-*Imperator* of the Hamburg America Line, sold to Cunard as reparation for the loss of the *Lusitania*) had joined the fleet and the *Caronia* slipped from the third to fourth largest of the Line's ships. But she was as popular as ever; she was still one of the 'Pretty Sisters'.

Below: Surrounded by 'Bum-Boats' the cruise passengers on board the must have purchased enough souvenirs to fill several suitcases.
Shipbuilding & Shipping Record

7

A Change of Routine

The 'Pretty Sisters' had been designed for the North Atlantic route to New York to carry the wealthy in First Class, the lucky in Second, the ordinary in Third and a mass of emigrants in Steerage. The United States had been taking the poor and the 'huddled masses' of Europe especially, for decades. After allowing millions free access to their country the Americans were starting, by degrees, to shut the door and become restrictive in who was allowed entry, so much so that the Americans proposed fining shipping companies $200 for each immigrant that exceeded a particular country's allotted annual quota.

The U.S. was so strict that 420 immigrants on the White Start Liner *Baltic* were refused entry and had to wait on Ellis Island (the Immigration Authority 'processing station') until the *Baltic* could return them to Britain at the shipping company's expense.

Alcohol prohibition was also at work in the United States and this would lead to cheap 'cruises to nowhere' when Americans booked a passage on a liner from New York out to sea and back to New York just to drink themselves silly outside territorial waters. These 'booze cruises' were the forerunners of today's popular past-time of cruising for everyone.

However, with the restrictions on immigration into the U.S. Cunard decided that the British Dominion of Canada would be an excellent place for emigrants to head for, and in December 1923 announced that sailings would be inaugurated between Liverpool, Belfast and Quebec. Previously, even from before the Great Potato Famine of the late 1840s – or the 'Great Starvation' as George Bernard Shaw had called it – Irish emigrants often had to travel to Liverpool to take passage on an emigrant carrier.

The service was planned to commence with the April thaw on the St. Lawrence river and the steamers chosen were the *Caronia* and *Carmania*. Because of the size of these liners, the largest and fastest to be placed on this route, passengers would be trans-shipped from Quebec to Montreal by train. During the St. Lawrence's 'closed season' Cunard's smaller ships, some specially built for the route such as the 'A' Class, would sail from Southampton via Cherbourg, Queenstown and Halifax, during which time the 'Pretty Sisters' would revert to the Liverpool–New York route. But before these new plans could develop the *Caronia* underwent major surgery for which she was sent to Vickers shipbuilding yard in Barrow, remaining there for three months between 5 January and 5 April 1924. 500 men would be locally employed on this work.

With newer, more modern liners plying the Atlantic and with less demand for First Class on the Canadian run, the 'Pretty Sisters' were converted from four classes to two, becoming Cabin and Third Class ships only. The old dormitories were swept away and smaller-occupancy berths were constructed in their place.

Below: Caronia entering Barrow shipyard in 1924 for a comprehensive refit.
Courtesy of the Sankey Collection (by kind permission of Jeffrey D. Sankey)

Above: A Cunard postcard shows 'Pretty Sisters' *Carmania* and *Caronia* together in Quebec.   *Charles A. Haas Collection*

Below: *Caronia* after her 1924 refit. Lifeboats are now double-banked, with additional boats aft on extended houses.   *Peter Newell Collection*

Another major change was to scrap her old coal-fired boilers and coal bunkers and replace them with oil-fired boilers and facilities to store oil-fuel. The change from coal to oil reduced the number of men required in the stokehold and the number of seamen on board was reduced to 480.

Another important change was to double the number of lifeboats that she carried. New davits were fitted and these carried double-banked boats. She now had twenty boats including two pairs in new locations above the deckhouse under her main mast and on her poop deck that had been extended forward. Her original sixteen boats had been insufficient ever since her build as the regulations at that time were themselves ten years out of date. They stated that a vessel of 10,000 tons or more (a large vessel at the time of the legislation) should carry sixteen boats. This was regardless of how many 'souls' the ship carried as the *Titanic* had found out at great cost. Even after this disaster the number of *Caronia*'s boats, or indeed the *Lusitania*'s for that matter, had not been increased.

The *Caronia* entered the Canadian trade sailing from Liverpool on 1 May 1924 arriving in Quebec on the 9th, returning via Queenstown. Her next voyage was by way of Belfast where apparently the facilities for passengers at the south end of the York Dock shed left much to be desired. She returned from Quebec through Queenstown.

This Canadian pattern kept up until November when calls were made into Newfoundland.

From November the *Caronia* transferred again to Liverpool – New York – Boston – Queenstown.

Luckily, 1925 was uneventful for the ship. Boston, Massachusetts, became a more regular destination, with a call being made before their arrival in New York. The *Caronia*'s short-lived Canadian service had come to an end as the numbers of emigrants did not justify the number of ships employed on the route. The Canadian Government at this time also asked for a 20% reduction

Above: *Caronia* pulling away from the Prince's Landing Stage at Liverpool. The famous Liverpool landmark the Liver
Building is on the right.   *NMGM, Merseyside Maritime Museum*

in immigrant fares and Cunard found it could not comply with this request. The trade later picked up but *Caronia* would not return to the service. New agreed fares for the 1927 season would be £2 from Liverpool to any of the Canadian ports. The previous passage ticket had cost £3! *Caronia* was scheduled for a more lucrative trade for that year.

Cunard realised too that many not-so-well-off Americans wanted vacations in Europe, so the liner stayed on the Atlantic for the whole of the year.

August saw Plymouth and Dover as the *Caronia*'s British ports-of-call, with London being used once again as the terminal for a single voyage. In October and November Plymouth, Cherbourg and Southampton became the liner's ports when she acted as a relief ship for whichever of the big three (*Aquitania*, *Berengaria* or *Mauretania*) was in overhaul.

A two-week January refit in Liverpool in 1926 began a year in which the improved facilities in le Havre allowed the port to replace Cherbourg as the French port of call. The *Caronia*'s year was spent on the 'Atlantic Ferry' with Liverpool, London or Southampton as the British terminal. Indeed, there was not much change in this schedule for the next two years. The *Caronia* continued to prove herself to be a most popular and profitable ship.

In 1927 the *Caronia* became part of a scheme that brought more Americans to Europe than at any other time since the Expeditionary Force in the Great War had been transported across the Atlantic. Several American organisations had charted an incredible thirteen Cunard steamers to bring members of their clubs and societies to various conventions and events in Great Britain and Europe during the year. The *Caronia* was booked in the first of these incredible events.

3,000 American and Canadian Rotarians wanted to attend a convention in Ostend between 4 and 10 June. Six liners of Cunard and the closely associated Anchor Line were hired to bring this large group across the Atlantic.

On Wednesday 25 May the 'Cunard Rotary Convoy' steamed out of New York harbour in one spectacular armada. The lead ship was the new *Carinthia* (she and the *Scythia* had pushed *Caronia* into sixth place in the Cunard largest ship list) and this ship had on board the president and high officers of Rotary.

During the course of the voyage the Rotarians kept in touch with each other by wireless. On the evening of 3 June the ships hove to off Dover to pick up North Sea pilots. Illuminated that night, the ships must have presented a magnificent sight.

The next morning the fleet, totalling 120,000 tons and extending over a mile, steamed through the Channel. The *Carinthia* (with Captain Diggle, ex-*Caronia*, in command) led, followed by the *Caronia* (now under the command of Captain Hossack), *Carmania*, *Lancastria*, *Samaria* and *Transylvania*.

Three of the vessels proceeded to Flushing where passengers were landed via cross-Channel steamers whilst the other three travelled on to Antwerp.

The second large convoy of the year brought American Legionnaires in September and the vessels involved this time were the *Scythia*, *Lancastria*, *Carmania*, *Tuscania*, *Antonia* and *Caledonia*. Other parties would use some of these ships plus the *Aurania* for their own excursions.

The North Atlantic, unlike other routes, had been very profitable in 1927.

The Havana Storm

At the end of 1927 (14 November) the *Caronia* was in Liverpool for an extended overhaul that would last for nearly three months. The hull and machinery of the 'Pretty Sister' must have been sound as it was considered viable to spend large amounts of money on the refit and alterations.

Caronia and *Carmania* were altered and reconditioned to cater for the new class rating of 'Tourist Third-Cabin', as well Third Class, which was designed to cater for the increasing number of 'ordinary' Americans wishing to holiday in Europe.

One of the bigger jobs of the overhaul was the fitting of new funnels, each weighing 26 tons and of a height of nearly 60 feet.

In the passenger accommodation new single and double cabins were provided for Cabin Class and the First Class and other cabins on the upper four decks had hot and cold running water plumbed in. Each bed in these cabins was now of mahogany and also had its own bedside reading light. New curtains, carpets and linoleum were provided increasing the comfort of the rooms. The old, fixed revolving dining chairs were replaced by armchairs in the Cabin Dining Room and the Smoking, Drawing and Writing Rooms and Lounge were repainted and refurbished.

Cabin Class rooms now had bathrooms and accommodation was now provided for 536 Cabin (formerly First); 222 Tourist and 404 Third, although 136 of the latter could be converted to Tourist if required. At last, the remaining large rooms had disappeared giving way to more private two-berth rooms.

In Third Class the old wooden decking in the Dining Room was tiled over with linoleum and the fixed, swivel seats were replaced by loose chairs. Seating was now at tables for 6, 8, 9 or 10. The areas previously occupied by Third Class lavatories were now used for stewards' accommodation.

The decks, too, took on new identities. The Promenade Deck became 'A' Deck; Shelter Deck became 'C'; Main – 'E'; Lower – 'F'; Upper – 'D'; and Bridge – 'B'.

Caronia was now ready to join her more modern fleet mates but she and her 'Pretty Sister' *Carmania* were still the fastest ships running out of Liverpool.

She remained on the Atlantic service for most of

Above: Painting the two new funnels at the end of the major overhaul of 1927–28. The funnels were 60 feet high and each weighed nearly 26 tons.
Shipbuilding & Shipping Record

1928, but when *Caronia* left London on 13 December it would be three-and-a-half months before she returned. She would be sailing into hotter waters in more ways than one.

A series of twelve six- or seven-night Winter Cruises had been planned for this month's sailing out of New York to Havana. Immediately she caused a stir amongst American politicians who, in the guise of the United States Shipping Board, put the *President Roosevelt* on the route as strong opposition to the *Caronia* and a rate war ensued.

This was a shame as two other American shipping companies had agreed to *Caronia* sailing to Cuba so long as she did not carry freight. The presence of the graceful Cunarder on the route helped greatly to develop Havana as a winter refuge for sun-hungry Americans.

Cunard stated that the cruises were so popular that, not only would the *Caronia* continue the Havana Winter Cruises but that her sister would also join her thus introducing a twice-weekly service. The Americans gave a 'knee-jerk' response and withdrew U.S. mails from three Cunard ships. On the insistence of the American Post Master General this instruction was soon rescinded.

Between the General Strike of 1926 (which did not really affect British Shipping) and the Great Depression of the late 1920s and early 1930s the average British working family led a meagre existence. To help compensate for this the Cunard Company held two Christmas parties in 1929 on board the *Caronia* for over a thousand of their dockside workers whilst the ship was berthed at the Huskisson Dock in Liverpool. The Christmas dinner was augmented by gifts of tobacco and cigarettes to each guest.

Sir Thomas Royden, Chairman of Cunard, gave a speech reminding the guests that foreign shipping companies received subsidies while Cunard and other British companies did not, but Cunard had to depend on its own resources to give 'the finest service in the world.'

Further statements in the new year would show that, although First and Second Class cabin occupancy was falling, there was a healthy rise in numbers travelling 'Tourist Third-Cabin, (42,000 in the past year)' which more than justified the sums spent on the 'Pretty Sisters.'

Above: Gone are the old Third Class Dining Room furnishings and a new 'Tourist Third-Cabin' room takes its place during the 1927–28 refit. *Shipbuilding & Shipping Record*

Left: After the Winter 1927-–28 refit smaller tables, new chairs and new decor grace the *Caronia*'s refurbished Cabin (First) Class Dining Room. Class names seem to be changed almost as often as the table linen! *Shipbuilding & Shipping Record*

Below: *Caronia* at Huskisson Dock, Liverpool in a picture that must date from 1905/6 as she still carries the vents that were removed shortly after her introduction into service. Here on board at Christmas 1929 Cunard gave two parties for over one thousand of their dockside workers. *Charles A. Haas Collection*

'... and Beauty Dwells in Them'

(J. M. W. Turner)

The beginning of 1931 saw only three cruises to Havana by the *Caronia* and then it was the London –Southampton–New York run until July.

For her penultimate cruise the *Caronia* would, unusually, sail from Southampton. Calls were made at Vigo, Gibraltar, Malta, Tangiers, Santa Cruz, Las Palmas, Tenerife, Madeira, returning to Southampton.

By now the 'Pretty Sisters' were 26 years old and old-fashioned when compared to the new Cunard ships and the art deco liners being built by other companies. Combined with a fall-off in trade due to the Great Depression the two ships did not have much of a future.

After the Mediterranean cruise the *Caronia* sailed on a two-week cruise to Norway, again from Southampton. On the way she called in at South Shields on the Tyne. There, passengers including Lord Kirkely, embarked on the liner from a steam ferry of the Tyne Improvement Commission as the ship lay inside the Tyne piers for about an hour in the afternoon.

Her fjord cruise included calls at Bergen, Molde and Trondheim and she returned via Lerwick to Liverpool.

The *Caronia*'s last commercial voyages were Liverpool –Queenstown–New York, returning to Southampton via Queenstown. Then Southampton direct to New York returning to London for the last time on 5 October 1931 via Plymouth and le Havre.

In August passenger rates had been drastically cut and cuts were being planned in merchant seamen's pay. Cunard made an announcement about the *Carmania*, so it can be supposed that the same also went for the *Caronia*: 'The *Carmania* is not going to be scrapped. She has just returned to London from New York. That is the last trip we intend to make with her this year. There is not enough work to justify keeping her in active service during the winter, and we shall not have sufficient use for her during the next few months.'

The *Carmania* was laid up in Gravesend but at least the *Caronia* was kept busy with her last two cruises. But finally, with the deepening Depression and a surplus of

Above: Sister ship *Carmania* arrives at Blyth in April 1932, where she is to be broken up by Hughes, Bolckow. *Caronia* similarly came to Blyth for breaking, but was sold on to Japan.
Shipbuilding & Shipping Record

Left: In the summer of 1931 *Caronia* made a one and only cruise to Norwegian waters. *En route* she called at the mouth of the Tyne on 30 July. Here, a Tyne ferry approaches the liner to embark passengers.
Frank & Sons

ships, the *Caronia* was sent to Sheerness on 14 October to sit out the bleak winter. On 27 January 1932 she was moved to the Great Nore Anchorage, eventually ending up at Blyth on 19 May.

She lay at Blyth for seven months. Her sister had come this way, too, and had been broken up by the shipbreaking firm of Hughes Bolckow and it was towards the hammers of this firm that *Caronia* was now directed, being bought by that company on 15 January.

The sale of the fading but still 'Pretty Sisters' – together at the end as they had been throughout their peacetime careers – was described as 'the largest scrap jobs of the year'

Because the date of purchase by Hughes Bolckow Shipbreaking Company of Blyth was four months earlier than the actual arranged delivery of the old ship the price increased by £2,000 to just over £20,000.

However, the *Caronia* was not to meet her end in Great Britain. The shipbreakers were made an offer that they could not refuse - £32,000 by the Japanese who planned to use the breaking of the ship in their country to 'check unemployment and to assist steel and associated trades.' (The latter probably meant using the ship's steel in the Japanese build-up of their navy).

Soon after the *Caronia* had been sold on to Japan some malicious damage occurred on board that resulted in investigations by the police. A quantity of acid was maliciously poured into four of the dynamos on the vessel causing an estimated £1,000 worth of damage.

Whoever the culprits and whatever their reasons, it did not delay the suffering liner's departure for long. She had been due to leave the waters of England on 20 December but her sailing was delayed for only a week and on 27 December, she left.

Above: 'Packing up' on the *Carmania* before disposal for breaking up. A similar scene must have occurred on the *Caronia* the following year.

Shipbuilding & Shipping Record

She had been struck from the British Register on 10 December and for her one-way trip to Japan she was renamed *Taiseiyo Maru*.

The old *Caronia* went via Dakar, Durban (where she had to return twice because of engine and boiler troubles) and Batavia (more machinery troubles), finally reaching her last landfall in Osaka on 28 March1932.

The 'Pretty Sisters' had together given nearly sixty years of service in peace and war and both would be remembered in other ships that would bear their names.

Below: Flying Japanese colours at her stern and with her new name at her bow, the *Taiseiyo Maru* awaits her end in Japanese waters near Osaka.
Alex Duncan/Peter Newell Collection

CARONIA (II)
The 'Green Goddess'
1949–1967

10
The Second Line

The second *Caronia* had her origin over a decade before she was built. In 1934 Cunard had merged with the White Star Line and a British government loan granted to the new Cunard-White Star Company enabled completion of the world's first 1000 foot liner – the fabled *Queen Mary* – and the building of her equally mighty sister the *Queen Elizabeth*, launched in 1940.

Cunard recognised, however, that there was still room on the North Atlantic for smaller passenger ships ('the second line' as Sir Percy Bates, Cunard-White Star chairman, described them) built and operated to complement the giant vessels.

These smaller ships were required for two reasons – first, to replace older ships of lesser tonnages and speeds and, second, to substitute for whichever of the giant *Queen*s might be in twice-yearly overhaul. The two proposed ships, to be known as 'intermediates', had therefore to be of sufficient size and speed to maintain an express Atlantic partnership when called upon to do so.

In July 1936, contracts to build the 'intermediates' were put out to tender: each was to be of around 32,000 tons gross with a speed of about 22 knots. It was suggested that they should be of an improved *Georgic* and *Britannic* design – the last two ships built for the independent White Star Line.

The contract for the first 'intermediate' was placed with Cammel Laird and Company, to be built at Birkenhead. When the keel of Yard No. 1029 was laid on Monday, 24 May 1937, it was announced that the liner would be placed on Cunard's transatlantic route between London, le Havre, Southampton and New York. In October it was announced that the new Cunarder

would take the name of an earlier ship that had, remarkably, kept the Blue Ribband (the speed record for the North Atlantic crossing) for over twenty years – the *Mauretania*. This earlier, magnificent four-funnelled ship, built in 1906, had had been scrapped in 1935 – an event almost of national mourning – during rationalisation of the recently combined Cunard and White Star fleets.

As the new *Mauretania* grew on the stocks, war clouds began to mar the optimism with which she was being built, as Britain became embroiled in a military build-up.

Cammel Laird had a big share of the naval shipbuilding programme that ensued. At Birkenhead, the battleship *Prince of Wales* and the submarine *Thetis* grew alongside the more peacefully intended *Mauretania* which was being built on the slipway recently vacated by the aircraft carrier *Ark Royal*.

The *Mauretania*, launched on 28 July 1938, by Lady Bates, wife of Sir Percy, was the largest ship to have then been built in England. At 771.5 feet long, 89.5 feet wide, she would eventually be measured at 35,739 gross tons. Her fitting-out took just under a year and, on Saturday 16 June 1939, she made her maiden voyage from Liverpool to New York. *Mauretania* made only two more transatlantic voyages before the Declaration of War in September 1939. Called-up into war service in 1940, she would serve until September 1946 transporting thousands of troops to theatres of war around the globe, bringing them home again after the War's end.

Only in 1947 did *Mauretania* return to her Cunard-White Star sailings, working in partnership with the two *Queen*s from Southampton. The second 'intermediate', conceived over 10 year earlier, had yet to join her.

'Number 635'

At the War's end the Cunard-White Star Line, as with many other shipping companies, wanted to replace the ships that they had lost during the years of conflict and to replace some of the surviving – but ageing and war-weary – units of their fleet with new, more modern tonnage.

In mid-1945, Sir Percy Bates announced his company's ambitious plans to build new ships with an aggregate gross tonnage of 76,000 and a total cost of £14.5 million. These plans included the construction of two cargo liners (eventually named *Asia* and *Arabia*); two combination vessels carrying 250 passengers as well as a substantial cargo load (*Media* and *Parthia*); and one passenger ship of the *Mauretania*-type, but 'slightly smaller'. Negotiations were by then already underway with shipbuilders John Brown and Company Limited, of Clydebank, Scotland, renowned builders of the *Queen Mary* and *Queen Elizabeth* and a contract to build the new passenger ship was signed towards the end of 1945.

The proposed new passenger ship was, as usual, given a shipyard reference number by which she would be known until a suitable name could be given to her. So the ship began her life as 'Number 635' (the 101st ship to be built at the Scottish shipyard since the *Queen Mary* had been launched in 1934). On St. Valentine's Day, 14 February 1946, the first keel plates for this were laid on the prepared wooden blocks that would support the ship during her building. Her overall length was to be 715 feet (665 feet between perpendiculars); her breadth 91 feet; draught of 30 feet; and a final tonnage of around 34,000 gross – or about 55 feet shorter; 16 inches wider and 1000 tons less than her erstwhile sister, the *Mauretania*.

Surprisingly, at a time when cargo space aboard ships was at a premium, No. 635 was to carry little or no cargo. She was being designed for, in those austere, immediate post-war days, a remarkable purpose – she was to go cruising, almost solely, to earn scarce dollars for a cash-starved Britain. As such, she was also being built for a relatively small number of passengers – around 900 in two classes when she was on the Atlantic run and 560 in one class (the number that could be seated in the two restaurants at one sitting) when she went cruising. She was the first ship to be designed for this dual role, with special attention placed on her cruising abilities.

No. 635 would be of sufficient speed to maintain, if so called upon, a North Atlantic service with whichever of the *Queens* was not undergoing their annual winter and summer overhaul.

Because of No. 635's unusual role and carrying capacities, a young assistant naval architect involved with the vessel's design was reported as saying: 'It takes a good naval architect to design a passenger ship that carries a lot of passengers; a good naval architect to design a cargo ship that carries lots of cargo; even better to design a ship that carries lots of passengers and cargo. But it takes a brilliant naval architect to design a passenger ship that carries hardly any passengers at all!'.

The arts, crafts and engineering skills of John Brown and Company's shipbuilding trades moved into action as the technical drawings of the ship were converted into full-scale lines on the Mould Loft floor. From these, the

Below left: 10.40 am St. Valentine's Day 1946, the keel plates of Yard No. 635 are laid.

Below right: Nine months later, to the day, the hull had been erected as far as having the beams of 'C' Deck in place. The shaft tunnel housings are in position and the stern casting that will house the rudder has been erected.

both National Archives of Scotland/Scottish Record Office

Above: Industry and agriculture side-by-side on the banks of the Clyde. Externally, the *Caronia* is almost ready for launching. Note that only a few windows along the Promenade Deck have been cut: this was to maintain structural strength during launch.   *courtesy of University of Liverpool Library*

curves of every frame would be faired and then used to shape forming moulds. The massive task of building started as the first one inch thick flat plates of the keel (doubled for the full extent of the outer flat plate keel) were rivetted together. Then the upright plates of the vertical keel rose from the flat plates and, on each side at specific spacings (generally 36 inches, reducing towards the bow and stern), vertical floors were erected – the dividing members of the double bottom which, when access openings had been cut into them, would form cellular double bottom tanks to be used for the storage of fuel oil and ballast, fresh and drinking water. At other specific intervals the floors would be made watertight with openings only for pipes, or access openings securely sealed with bolted manhole plates – and these would be the basis of the ten transverse watertight bulkheads. Pipes were manufactured and joined within the double bottom spaces to carry fuel, water and ballast, pumped to where it was required. From the floors' outer ends frames, the ribs of the ship were erected, true to within a fraction of an inch. The outer edges of the frames presented fair, smooth curves that, when plated over, would make the ship compatible to the easy flow of her natural environment – the sea. To ensure a smooth flow of water over the outer bottom below the waterline the edges of the overlapping plates, once rivetted into position, would be faired using patented 'Aranbee', a cement-type compound.

Onto the frames' inner edges brackets were rivetted brackets to support the outer ends of the beams that would, in turn, support the various decks. There would be ten of these, two within the superstructure – Sports (which incorporated the Boat Deck) and Sun Decks. Within the hull would be Promenade; Main; 'A'; Restaurant (or 'R') Deck; 'B'; 'C' and 'D' Decks, and the Tank Top which essentially provided the seatings for the engines and boilers. Decks were separated from each

other by four transverse rows of tubular pillars, many of which would be covered with decorative panelling where they appeared in public rooms.

Meanwhile, other items were being produced for the new Cunarder. Firms from all over Great Britain and its Empire were manufacturing components that would be included in or on the ship. Great steel forgings were cast in Darlington and transported to the shipyard. The stem casting, with its elegant clipper-like curve, would form the bow (the last Cunarder to carry a clipper bow was the *Batavia* of 1870), other castings formed the cruiser stern and rudder post and others would support the propeller shafts. Turbine engines and boilers were built in John Brown's own Engine Shops; two 22-ton, four-bladed 'Scimitar' propellers of almost 19 feet in diameter were cast, honed and polished by the Manganese Bronze and Brass Company of Birkenhead. Six 45 foot long, 15 foot wide, single-screw motor launches fitted with deck shelters fore and aft and complete with toilet, eight conventional motor lifeboats and two emergency boats, were built in rivetted aluminium by Hugh McLean and Sons. The motor launches, propelled by Thornycroft R.L.6 diesel engines, were to ferry sixty passengers ashore when the liner had to anchor offshore during a cruise. Three anchors (including one spare), each weighing 18 tons, were cast, as were the $3^1/4$ inch diameter links that would make up the lengths of the anchor cable chains. Chairs, tables, 1200 doors, panelling, soft-furnishings and carpets, light-fittings, 700 telephones, 570 'slave' clocks (these, at a touch of a button on the Bridge, could be corrected for changes in time zone, all controlled by a master chronometer) and auxiliary machinery for refrigeration, ventilation, electricity generation, pumping, etc., were made by contractors all over the country and Empire.

By March 1947, a name had been decided upon for No. 635. She was to be called – *Caronia*.

12

'The Heir to a Great Reputation'

In the immediate post-war years building materials, such as steel, were very scarce and special government permission had to be sought to obtain sufficient materials with which to build ships like the *Caronia*. Because of her potential importance to Britain's economy permits were granted and supplies of steel were made available, as were other essential materials such as scarce woods. When the *Queen Elizabeth* had been refitted after the War there had been an outcry in some quarters that equipment that could have been used to rebuild houses was being diverted to provide luxury for those who could afford to travel. Cunard responded that almost all the material required for the *Queen* had been provided before the War and had been kept in storage until it could once again be used for its intended purpose. The detractors were silenced, and remarkably remained quiet as material was made available for the *Caronia*. Perhaps it was the Cunard's well-publicised patriotic intention to use the ship as a dollar earner for Britain that kept the erstwhile critics silent.

By late 1947, the ship was well advanced in her construction and a launch date had been finalised. It was to be on Thursday 30 October and Her Royal Highness Princess Elizabeth, had been invited to perform the ceremony. This would be the last public function that Her Royal Highness would undertake in the weeks before her marriage to the dashing young Lieutenant Philip Mountbatten, who would accompany his bride-to-be to Clydeside for the occasion. The Lieutenant's uncle, Lord Mountbatten of Burma, until two months previously Viceroy of India, would also accompany the royal party.

The launching of *Caronia* would provide the occasion for Princess Elizabeth's third visit to the shipyard. She had accompanied her mother, H.M. the Queen, to the yard when Queen Elizabeth had launched her namesake in 1938 and the Princess had returned on a second occasion on her own to launch the battleship *Vanguard* in 1944.

On *Caronia*'s launch day a great number of people congregated in the shipyard to witness the launching of the ship brightly and uniquely painted in a pastel green, and to see the Princess before her wedding. On arrival the royal party was greeted and escorted through the cordoned crowd by the shipyard manager, John Rannie. The launch platform was gaily covered in red, white and blue bunting for the occasion. The party ascended the approach ramp to the platform and the Princess and the Lieutenant halted at its outer corner whilst the National Anthem was played, the Princess standing still and solemn whilst her fiancé saluted in best naval tradition.

The couple then moved to the front centre of the platform beneath which hung the Union flag.

Near to the time of the launch the weather tried to spoil the event but, despite heavy rain showers during the most critical times, it did not dampen the enthusiasm of the crowd.

The usual order of launches was altered on this occasion and the new chairman of Cunard, Frederic A. Bates, brother of Sir Percy who had died on the eve of the *Queen Elizabeth*'s first post-war voyage, delivered a speech of welcome to the Princess who then in response, said:

> "I am so happy that on this, my third visit, my future husband is by my side. He has served with the Royal Navy in war and in peace, so that I need not dwell on his love of the sea and all that belongs to it. Naturally, he shares my interest in your achievements and my pride in the fame which our designers and builders have won for us throughout the ages, and which will be given new life in this new ship.
> "Every man and woman in these islands knows how great a part shipping has played in the establishment and maintenance of our national greatness.
> "In our own times those swift and graceful giants, the *Queen Mary* and the *Queen Elizabeth*, have gripped the imagination of the peoples on both sides of the Atlantic.
> "The *Caronia* is thus the heir to a great reputation, a reputation which has been gained in our shipyards, by no means least in that of John Brown and Company.
> "Our Merchant Navy, for its part, has never taken second place to that of any nation. The Cunard-White Star Line, under whose famous flag the *Caronia* will sail, has played a very great part in winning these laurels for our country."

She continued, making what became a rather longer than usual speech for a launch.

Right: Before moving to centre platform where she will perform the launching ceremony, H.R.H. Princess Elizabeth pauses at the platform's outer corner as the National Anthem in played. Lieutenant Philip Mountbatten executes an exemplary Naval salute by her side.   *courtesy of University of Liverpool Library*

Left: Touching the water for the first time, the Cunard-White Star liner *Caronia* is almost waterborne. Her hull, for the time being, is painted in one shade of light green.
courtesy of University of Liverpool Library

built up a momentum to hit the water with a splash.

Tugs busily and carefully arranged themselves around the newly waterborne hull and escorted the ship to her fitting-out jetty where she was berthed. There she would remain until fully fitted with engines, boilers and every other fitting that would transform her from a green painted steel shell into a superb ocean liner.

After the launch the Princess was presented with a large bouquet and she and the large party of guests took lunch in the specially adapted Tracing Office within the yard. During the lunch, a ration-breaking affair of cream of tomato soup; cold turkey, ham and tongue; croquette potatoes and green peas; Pear Melba followed by coffee; Lord Aberconway, chairman of John Brown and Company, proposed a toast: "Success to T.S.S. *Caronia* and her owners Cunard-White Star Limited" and presented a set of silver George II fluted dishes to the Princess. In his reply, Mr Fred Bates referred to a scheme which had been sent to him describing an inventor's idea for fast, jet-engined aircraft that used space –'cabinjectiles' – that "will leave here (Britain) after breakfast and arrive in New York before lunch!" (laughter). Lord Aberconway had also made mention of the last time that the Princess had visited the shipyard when she had come alone. He said that "Today there is one difference – she does not come alone." Apparently this statement brought smiles from both the Princess and Lieutenant Mountbatten and drew forth a burst of applause from the guests and a 'vigorous thumping of the tables.'

On completion of the Princess's speech, Sir Stephen Piggott, Managing Director of the shipyard, quietly indicated which button to press. H.R.H. said a few words naming the ship and pressed the launch button. As a bottle of wine broke against the curving bow of the *Caronia*, the ship seemed reluctant to test her new freedom but, after a pause of almost thirty seconds, the first slight riverwards movement was detected until she

Left: With lines abeam and ahead, the newly launched *Caronia* is carefully pulled into her fitting out berth. The liner alongside is New Zealand Lines *Rangitiki* undergoing a major refit after war service as a troopship.
courtesy of University of Liverpool Library

13

Four Shades of Green

The late autumn of the launch turned into winter and, on occasion, snow would cover the liner's upper decks. Internal stiffening, introduced to strengthen the ship for the stresses of the launch, was removed and the enormous task to finish *Caronia* recommenced with a renewed vigour. 600 joiners along with electricians, boiler makers, engine fitters and a host of other highly skilled trades joined the shipwrights, platers, plumbers, welders, etc., bringing the labour force working on the ship to a total of up to 3,000.

Large windows were cut into the hull along what would become the enclosed Promenade Deck and Bridge front areas. These had been left as solid plate to retain some integral strength against the stresses of launching.

Within caverns that would become public rooms, roughly hewn tree-trunks supported deckheads where lavish pillars would eventually be placed. Organised chaos disguised the intensive work in hand. However, an overall plan was in action. As additional supports and superstructure were added in the joiners' and other shops in the yard, carefully finished fittings and decorations were being manufactured to create a luxury only dreamt of by a British public still living under the austere conditions of rationing in post-war Britain.

On first sight of the new liner, the observer's attention was immediately drawn to the colour of the yacht-like lines of the hull. The *Caronia* was painted a shade of light green instead of in the usual Cunard livery of black above the waterline (as earlier publicity pictures had depicted her). During the later stages of her completion this single, overall scheme of green would be changed to four different shades of the colour.

This paint had been rigorously tested for eighteen months. Steel plates had been coated with the colour and placed on the foredecks of two other Cunard ships as they travelled to climates ranging from freezing to tropical. It proved to be hard-wearing, did not fade as some greens did to a pale blue, and also reflected sunlight thus helping to keep the ship cool in hot climes. (Another aid to temperature control was achieved by spraying the inside of the hull plates with an asbestos compound which kept the heat within the ship in cold regions and the heat out in hotter ones). The green paint also cut down the glare of the sun reflected by white paint used on previous cruise liners.

Top: Detail from a postcard of a painting by C. E. Turner of the 'Green Goddess' showing her unusual colour scheme.
David Hutchings Collection

Right: *Caronia* lying alongside her fitting-out berth as workmen busily throng the jetty.   *Cunard*

Above: Like fitting together pieces of a giant jig-saw, joiners cover one of the pillars in the First Class Smoke Room with its polished veneer. The column's reverse and base lie alongside ready for attention. The ceiling has yet to be finished. Relief panels depicting Anglo-Saxon representations of the months of the year pressure-formed in Bakelite-impregnated paper were fixed at the outer edges of the twelve-sided ceiling motif. At first, the fluorescent lighting in the ceiling had an unflattering effect on ladies' make-up. *courtesy of University of Liverpool Library*

The dashing, but nonchalant, chairman of W. & J. Leigh, the manufacturers of the paint, later described his company's pastel green product to the *New Yorker* magazine as "a new plastic sort of thing, a triumph of the science of colour dynamics." He declined to give away the formula of the paint – "trade secret and all that rot." The liner's launch colour of one shade of green was apparently the original finished scheme, but a graded colouring was later adopted to give the ship a 'tapered look'.

The styling of the four shades of green began above the white ribbon of the waterline which surmounted the underwater red-painted boot-topping of the ship's outerbottom. The first shade of light green was applied to the main hull and this was terminated by a twelve-inch ribbon of darker green which extended around the hull at the level of 'A' Deck. Above the ribbon another shade of green, but lighter than that of the hull, was applied up to Boat Deck level. Deckhouses, derrick posts and mast would be painted in an even lighter shade.

Inside the hull, bare steel was coated with red lead before being finished with the paint scheme or other décor appropriate to that area of the vessel. Temporary structures were replaced by permanent structures to support decorative features such as columns of highly polished rare wood veneers. The ship's structural pillars were also decoratively disguised in passenger areas.

Cabin bulkheads were constructed and electrical wiring and plumbing installed. All First Class and, uniquely, some Cabin Class cabins had bathrooms *en suite*. The First Class cabins even had taps that dispensed chilled water – a great favourite with American travellers. Once piping and electrical wiring had been installed, false ceilings and walls in various finishes were fitted, all to a high standard.

Gradually, under the sharp eyes of their foremen, the craftsmen and labourers were skillfully transforming a floating industrial site into a ship of luxury.

The Power Behind the *Caronia*

The 34,000 tons of luxury that was the *Caronia*, and the 900 passengers that would sail in her, had to be transported across the Atlantic and around the world with a regularity and reliability that would establish a reputation for punctuality at every port that she visited. To be transported efficiently meant to be driven reliably, and to enable the *Caronia* to do this her propulsion plant – turbine engines and boilers – had to be of the best. She was fitted, it was hoped, with just this.

Since the introduction of the turbine engine into the Cunard fleet after the grand experiment with the 'Pretty Sisters,' *Carmania* and the first *Caronia* in 1905, the use of this means of propulsion had been used in other faster units of the fleet with an increasing efficiency.

The second *Caronia* was provided with two sets of the most up-to-date design of the Parsons impulse reaction geared turbine. The thousands of stainless steel impulse blades were fitted individually into the grooves in the rotor and cylinder throughout the turbines. The reaction blades were of stainless iron. Turbines and boilers had been built in the shipyard's own shops.

The turbines took their steam from six Yarrow-type water-tube boilers at an initial pressure of 550 p.s.i. (gauge) which was delivered at a temperature of 780°F.

The boilers were hoisted aboard at the fitting-out jetty and were arranged in three pairs in the single Boiler Room. Each side-fired boiler contained five drums, one of which acted as the superheater header. Four of the boilers each had a heat generating surface of 8,387 square

feet and a superheating surface of 2,945 square feet. The remaining two boilers each had a generating surface of 5,681 square feet and superheating surfaces of 2,224 square feet. In the larger boilers the normal evaporation was 86,000 pounds of steam per hour and, in the smaller, 50,000 pounds. The steam was delivered to the boilers at 600 p.s.i. (gauge) at a temperature of 800°F. Each boiler contained 14,000 tubes and their firebricks were laid after the boilers had been lifted on board. Two bricklayers laid the bricks whilst a labourer kept them supplied with materials.

Each main turbine set comprised one high, one intermediate and one low-pressure turbine driving the main gear wheel via double reduction gearing. The gearing would cause *Caronia*'s Engineers quite a few headaches in the years to come and it was sometimes said that, because of frequent filing of gear teeth, a *Caronia* Engineer could be easily identified from the lack of skin on his knuckles!

The reduced size of the high-pressure turbine which could be fitted at the increased revolutions possible with the type of double reduction gearing used, was a great advantage at the adopted high steam pressures and temperatures encountered.

Right: Set out in the yard's workshops, the two set of main turbines and gearing can be clearly seen.

Below: *Caronia's* Boiler Room housed six side-fired five drum Yarrow water-tube boilers that provided 50,000 pounds of steam per hour.

Shipbuilding & Shipping Record

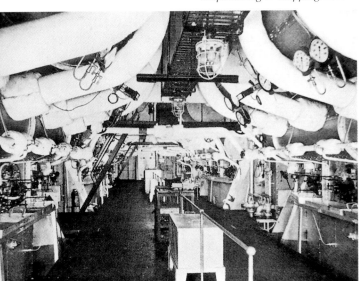

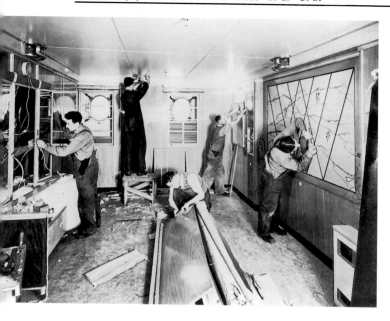

Above: Shipyard craftsmen fit out a first class bedroom on Main Deck. This was part of one of the luxury suites that had an adjoining private sitting room. Notice how the ship's portholes are covered over from the inside with false sash windows. A very similar room fully fitted and furnished can be seen below. *Cunard*

Below: A bedroom in one of the deluxe suites on Main Deck, one of eight such cabins. The 'sash windows' now completely disguise the portholes beneath. *Cunard*

Each of the intermediate and low-pressure turbines drove a separate pinion, which engaged directly with the main gear wheel. For going astern, a single three-row impulse high-pressure turbine was incorporated in each of the intermediate ahead-turbine casings. A single three-row impulse low-pressure stage was incorporated in each of the low pressure ahead turbines.

At full power, the high-pressure turbine would run at 3,686 r.p.m., while the intermediate and low-pressure turbines ran at 1,990 r.p.m. The gearing reduced these high speeds at the turbines to 140 r.p.m. at the propeller. A trials speed of 24 knots and a service speed of 22 knots would subsequently be achieved.

Gradually within the hull, compartments were fitted and finished with the equipment or décor necessary for that compartment to meet its function. There were compartments to assist in the technical functioning of the ship, its navigation and its catering. Catering alone required an enormous space for stores (dry, wet, bottled, barrelled, chilled, kosher, etc.) and areas for the preparation and cooking of the food as well as sculleries for washing up. Crew members ate what the passengers ate, but the Stewards, especially, sometimes had to eat standing in the galleys. Messes were available for Waiters and Engineers but senior staff ate in the Restaurants at allotted tables.

The needs of the prospective passenger were luxuriously met for sleeping, dining, recreation and relaxing. First Class staterooms and cabins were, of course, the most well-appointed. On the Main Deck, just forward of amidships, six luxury suites were provided, three port and three starboard. Two large suites each comprised two twin bedrooms, an interconnecting

Left: This sitting room in one of the Main Deck deluxe suites is luxuriously fitted with the very best of contemporary late 1940s design.   *Cunard*

sitting room and a single berth cabin which could be used by a maid or valet. The other four suites each had a twin bedroom, their own sitting room, and could be interconnected if necessary.

Two-berthed suite M36, for example, was decorated with gull-grey walls and a shell-pink ceiling. The bed recess was panelled in beige leather with vertical dividers of honey-coloured sycamore. Drawer fronts were covered in cream leather and a specially woven royal blue carpet was partially covered with rugs in grey, beige and blue, reflecting the overall scheme of the room. The sitting room of suite M38 had flame coloured maple walls with gilt-metal trim. The furniture was in a tawny coachwood, also with gilt trim. The beige carpet was enhanced by a sage green circular rug and curtains at the windows, some of which were sash operated, were of turquoise silk. The quilted upholstery was in a soft fawn with pastel floral tapestry.

The cabins had hot and cold ventilation and heaters for colder climes. Full air-conditioning in cabins would not be introduced until a later refit.

A First Class entrance was just forward of these suites and the Purser's Office was aft of this entrance so the occupants of the suites did not have far to walk to make enquiries, exchange currencies or prepare to board one of the shore-bound motor launches. Other First Class accommodations were on Sun Deck, 'A' and 'R' Decks – very handy for the Restaurants!

Hairdressing (the men's barbers would be called 'Tyme For Men') and beauty salons on the centreline amidships were also on Main Deck, mainly given over to First Class accommodation. There were Cabin Class

cabins aft (some of which could be converted to First Class accommodation for cruises.) The Cabin Class Cocktail Bar and Lounge, sited far aft, gave out onto the Cabin Class promenade deck. Part of this Cabin Class public area could be partitioned off to form a Cruise and entertainment's office operated by Thomas Cook and Son during World Cruises. When partitioned, the remaining lounge and cocktail bar were referred to as the Raleigh Room. Apparently, Thomas Cook staff using the office had to be careful of what they discussed as the partition was very thin and passengers in the Raleigh Room could possibly overhear their conversations!

At the end of July 1949, at the John Brown and Company Annual General Meeting in London, chairman Lord Aberconway said, "It is with regret that we have to report a substantial loss incurred in the building of the TSS *Caronia."* He went on to say that the construction of the ship had been delayed by the necessity of getting the *Queen Mary* and *Queen Elizabeth* back into service. This, combined with a rise in the cost of materials and some labour difficulties, necessitated a transfer from reserves from profits to cover contingencies of "£250,000 towards the loss made on the *Caronia."*

By the last week of August the *Caronia* was ready to receive the top section of what would be her most distinguishing feature – her funnel. Publicists were ready to inform the public that this would be the largest funnel fitted to any ship, larger even, than those fitted to the *Queen Elizabeth.* The last funnel section formed the wide black band that surmounted the famous red-with-black-bands funnel of the Cunard Line. It weighed 15 tons. The funnel was elliptical in section: 53 feet 9 inches

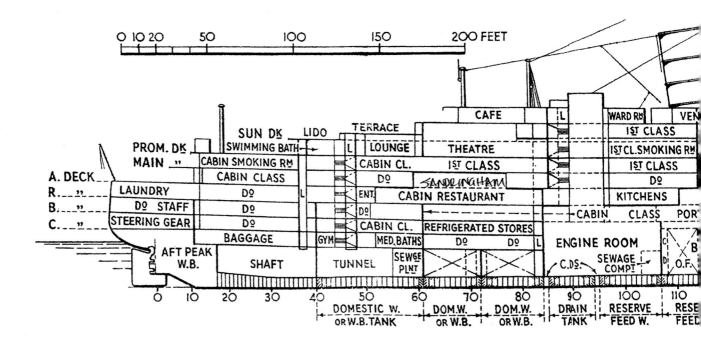

Above: A sectional elevation of *Caronia*'s profile showing the arrangement of the ship along the middle line.

Shipbuilding & Shipping Record

long, 26 feet 6 inches wide and had a height of 46 feet. Because the liner would have only one mast, the funnel would also house navigation lights (one electric and one oil) and two 'Tyfon' whistles which had an audible range of 6½ miles. To obviate any external supporting guys the funnel was stiffened internally, and it contained exhaust vents and dust extractors (of the wet-type) to remove soot particles from the exhaust smoke, keeping the after decks and passengers' clothing free of smuts. The total weight of funnel and machinery would be 125 tons. Completed, the funnel would dominate the sleek hull, perhaps making the ship rather squat in her final appearance. Awesome though the funnel was, its large expanse would prove to be problematic on more than one occasion in the coming years.

Work continued as deck planking was laid to cover promenade, sunning and sports decks and caulked in an age old tradition using special irons and hammers. Large square ventilation intakes were hoisted aboard; boat davits and derrick posts were fitted, all helping to complete the liner's exterior appearance. The davits that housed the special launches were, again, the largest to be fitted on a ship.

At about this time the hull of the ship was painted experimentally in the four shades of green, which once adopted, would make the *Caronia* recognisable wherever she went.

Yet another trademark of *Caronia*, her unusual tripod mast, was lifted on-board in three sections. The central tall section, the mast itself, held the Crow's Nest and navigational lights, and the two shorter sections served as support poles. The mast, 127 feet 6 inches above deck

level, was sited aft of the Navigating Bridge to enable the navigators to obtain a clear, uninterrupted view ahead.

In fitting out the hull, the needs of the officers and crew (of whom there were 587 in total) were also being met. The Captain and Navigating Officers were berthed on the Sports Deck in accommodation beneath the Wheelhouse; Quartermasters and Bos'uns were on 'A' Deck forward; Greasers and Firemen on 'R' Deck forward, forward of their cabins was a crew's Recreation Room and Bar. This was known as the 'Forward Pig', named after one of Liverpool's oldest pubs, the 'Pig and Whistle.'

The Masters-at-Arms', Stewards' and Engineers' cabins and messes were forward on 'B' Deck whilst Musicians, Laundry and Catering staff were accommodated aft. Portside, aft, housed male and female passenger hospitals, infectious wards, an operating theatre, dispensary and a separate hospital for the crew. There were Cabin Class cabins aft on this deck as on 'C' Deck below. Stewards were messed forward on 'C', the lowest of the accommodation decks, in 2, 4, 6 or 8-berth cabins (all looked after by their own 'Glory Hole' stewards) and their Recreation Room and Bar (the lower 'Pig and Whistle') was aft and starboard of their accommodation. Because 'C' Deck was very near to the waterline a regulation for both passengers and crew stipulated that the portholes here could be opened while *Caronia* was in port but that they must be secured when the ship was at sea.

During *Caronia*'s final weeks of completion, various artists would travel to Clydeside to supervise the installation and to make last minute changes or adjustments to their pieces, ensuring that their works, in

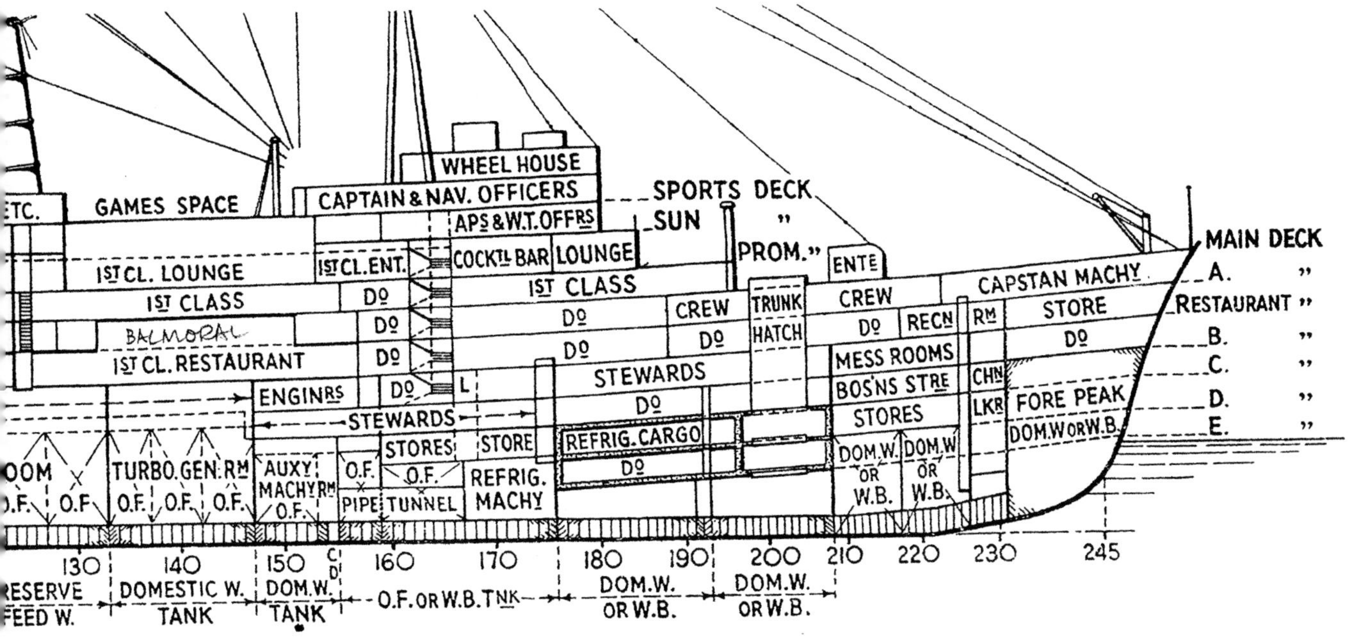
ETC.
GAMES SPACE
CAPTAIN & NAV. OFFICERS
WHEEL HOUSE
SPORTS DECK
SUN
PROM.
APS & W.T. OFFRS
1ST CL. LOUNGE
1ST CL. ENT.
COCKTL BAR
LOUNGE
1ST CLASS
1ST CLASS
DO
CREW
TRUNK
HATCH
ENTE
CREW
DO
RECN
RM
STORE
CAPSTAN MACHY
BALMORAL
1ST CL. RESTAURANT
STEWARDS
MESS ROOMS
BOS'NS STRE
STORES
CHN LKR
FORE PEAK
DOM.W OR W.B.
ENGINRS
STEWARDS
STORES
STORE
REFRIG. CARGO
O.F.
REFRIG. MACHY
TURBO. GEN. RM
AUXY. MACHY RM
PIPE TUNNEL
DOM.W. OR W.B.
MAIN DECK
A.
RESTAURANT
B.
C.
D.
E.
130
140
150
160
170
180
190
200
210
220
230
245
RESERVE FEED W.
DOMESTIC W. TANK
DOM.W. TANK
O.F. OR W.B. TNK
DOM.W. OR W.B.
DOM.W. OR W.B.

painted panels or murals, carved wood, etched glass, cast metal and other mediums were secured and correctly sited. For some reason, horses, both real and mythical, seemed to be a favourite subject amongst the artists and appeared in carvings as well as in paintings for cabins and public rooms alike.

By November 1948, Cunard announced that the captain who would take *Caronia* on her maiden voyage would be Captain Donald W. Sorrell. Respected by passengers and many crew alike he was known as 'Doddy' to his friends and as 'The Mighty Atom' to those who served under him because of his slight stature. In later years his wife, Isobel, would remember that he was 5 foot 6 inches but wanted to be 6 foot 3! Trained and certified as a Master in sail, Donald Sorrell joined Cunard in 1918 as a junior officer, the same year in which he obtained his Extra Master's and wedding certificates! Prior to being given command of *Caronia*, Captain Sorrell had been in command of the *Samaria*. A proficient artist, he had illustrated a book for passengers on basic seamanship written by James Bisset.

Captain Sorrell's Staff Captain would be Captain W. B. Tanner and his Chief Engineer Mr Douglas Horsburgh, a much respected ex-White Star engineer; Purser R. H. Newcombe and Chief Steward George Baker would head other departments.

The maiden voyage of Cunard's beautiful green liner with the 'new look' was now set for Tuesday 4 January 1949.

Below: This picture from a Cunard information sheet on the *Caronia* illustrates the immense size of the funnel. The cut-away shows some of the smoke uptakes (from the six boilers), fans and dust collectors (to trap soot). Ladders and platforms within the funnel give access to the different levels inside. On more than one occasion the size of *Caronia*'s funnel led her into difficulties as it would act like a sail when caught by the wind. The picture also shows the 20-ton diesel launches on their davits. The launches were used to ferry passengers ashore, sixty at a time. *Cunard*

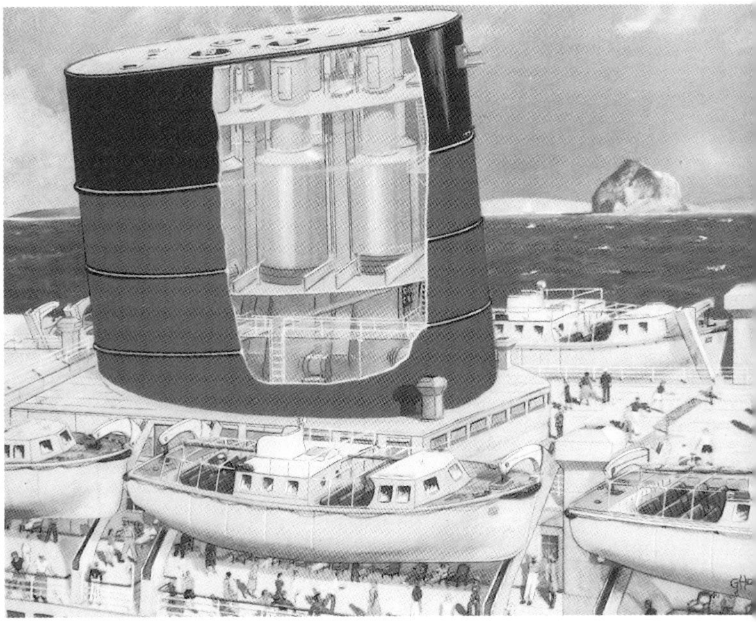

15
'The Gorgeous Palace'
(The Tempest, Act IV, Sc. 1)

aronia's main public rooms were comfortable, luxurious and the jewel in her crown. The highest of these rooms was the Verandah Bar, aft on the Sports Deck. Furnished with tables for two or four, it was an intimate place at night when its own orchestra was playing for dancing within or, in warm weather, outside on the open terrace. The ceiling was emblazoned with a stylised sun surrounding a central light; panelling was in a light wood; columns were tubular and chairs were in red upholstery on a light wooden frame.

The Verandah Bar's terrace led down to the 24 foot by 16 foot swimming pool, which was on a level of its own surrounded by a lido area.

Also on the Sports Deck was a large open area between the funnel and the Bridge where deck games such as deck tennis could be played.

From the Promenade Deck steps led onto an open promenade and deck games area for Cabin Class passengers on two-class voyages. Going forward on port and starboard sides were covered promenade areas, again Cabin Class. Doors here, flanked by potted palms, opened into Garden Lounges. With blue-painted wicker furniture and small, square glass-topped tables on linoleum floors the Garden Lounges were ideal places to relax after games on the outer decks. The forward doors led out into the First Class enclosed promenade deck, which gave this deck its name.

On Promenade Deck were most of the public rooms. Between the Cabin Class covered promenades and the shared Garden Lounges were the Cabin Class Lounge and the Cinema Theatre.

The Cabin Class Lounge was panelled with light woods. Small, round tables and armchairs in various reds or light green patterns sat on a floor a salmon-coloured linoleum decorated with widely spaced ribbons in green and yellow. Carpets were placed in the seating areas leaving the linoleum exposed in the walkways. A recess aft, with entrance doors from a lobby aft, contained a grand piano and room for a small band.

Forward of this lounge was the Cinema. Almost egg-shaped in plan, tapering towards the screen its walls, in polished walnut, were of an undulating design. Unlike many ocean liners which had stackable chairs, the seats were fixed, upholstered and had tip-up arms. The screen itself was surrounded in a deep moulding of white sycamore. When the liner was on the North Atlantic run,

Left: Seating around 285, the Cinema Theatre had First Class entrances forward and Cabin Class aft. Roughly egg-shaped in plan, all the occupants had a good view of the screen from their sprung seats with tip-up arms.

Inset: The polished walnut walls and red upholstered, blue-backed seats made the Cinema Theatre a richly coloured room.

both Cunard

Above: The Smoking Room in First Class (see also picture page 38) fully fitted with its unusual ceiling and lighting.

Right: The Writing Room was on the Promenade Deck port side between the First Class Smoking Room and Main Lounge, making a quiet retreat from the social activity in both rooms.

Below: The Observation Lounge Cocktail Bar was surrounded on three sides by the Observation Lounge which overlooked the ship's bow.

all Cunard

Left: Verandah Bar aft on Sports Deck with its striking central ceiling motif. This picture looks aft towards the stage where the *Caronia* Orchestra played to a very high standard for dancing. *Cunard*

figured veneer. Between each column a pale, golden mottled Canadian maple veneer concealed the edge and underside of the deck above the one-deck high side bays of the lounge. The veneer was repeated on the full height of the wall at the after end, forming a panel against which hung a photographic portrait of H.R.H. Princess Elizabeth and Lieutenant Philip Mountbatten. This would be replaced during the liner's first year of service by a portrait of the royal couple painted in oils by Edward Halliday. Below the portrait was another grand piano and room for a full band. A peach carpet, patterned with knot-shaped motifs separated by wavy ribbons of red and white, covered the floor and on this chairs covered in green, peach and fawn were arranged around small, circular tables.

Forward of the Main Lounge from a foyer a grand stairway led up to the Promenade Deck and down to the First Class Restaurant three decks below. Beyond the foyer lay the Observation Lounge Cocktail Bar, surrounded forward and on each side by the Observation Lounge itself which looked over the bows and gave views over the port and starboard quarters. The Cocktail Bar was a cool room hung with pale blue curtains with white horizontal stripes; light finished columns; a dark-fronted bar with red and light-blue leather barstools and chairs in peach and red placed at small round tables.

On Main Deck, below, the only major public room was the Cabin Class Smoke Room and Cocktail Bar.

From Main Deck one had to travel down two decks to find the two restaurants. Separated amidships by the large kitchens and ancillary stores, sculleries, larders, etc., the after Cabin Class restaurant was called the Sandringham, and the forward First Class restaurant the Balmoral.

Cabin Class passengers could use the Cinema at certain times. The forward end of the Cinema had doors for First Class passengers to enter from two short corridors port and starboard. The Library was situated off the portside corridor. With a glazed wall and door into the corridor, the windowless Library had 1,250 books lining the other three sides.

The two corridors entered the First Class Smoking Room. A very striking compartment, its main feature was the twelve-sided central ceiling motif with a large light fitting at its middle. The ceiling comprised four moulded sections each lit at its sides by fluorescent lamps. (These lamps initially caused problems with ladies' make-up making them look quite 'off-colour' – a suggestion in the technical press recommended coating the lamps with a pink wash!)

The outer edges of the moulded ceiling had been formed from paper impregnated with Bakelite resin and subjected to a hydraulic pressure of 5,000 tons. Each panel contained a design, by E. P. Thompson, based on Anglo-Saxon depictions of the months of the year. The ceiling was supported by four columns of a 'rounded triangular' section. A brick and tile fireplace with marble shelf adorned one end of the Smoking Room, backed by a wall of green bronze plate. A carpet of traditional design covered the floor and armchairs and settees were upholstered in crimson and black with a cream piping.

From the Smoking Room two short corridors took passengers forward past, on the port side, a comfortable, open-fronted Writing Room with fourteen desks.

These corridors then opened into the magnificent 72 feet long Main Lounge with two-deck-high ceiling. Tall columns here were hugely boxed-in with horizontally

Right: Looking forward over the *Caronia*'s bows, the Observation Lounge followed the curvature of the Bridge front. The small balustrade on the right led to doors that opened into the Observation Cocktail Bar. *Cunard*

Both restaurants were of similar size and layout, the Balmoral being 93 feet long and 54 feet wide. The central part of each room rose through two decks. Fully air-conditioned, as were the other public rooms, neither restaurant had natural lighting as, on the other side of their outer bulkheads, were corridors and cabins. 280 diners could be seated in each restaurant at tables for 2, 4, 6 or 8.

Dining chairs in both restaurants were of the same design but those in the Balmoral were upholstered in blue hide and those in the Sandringham in burgundy. The Balmoral was finished in a lighter veneer than the Sandringham, but both rooms were finished to a very high standard, as both would be used during cruising for one passenger class. Four large etched glass panels by John Hutton representing the Four Seasons adorned the walls of the centrum of the Sandringham. Both rooms had linoleum floor, increasing the sense of coolness when cruising in the tropics.

Apparently, the more distinguished passengers were seated at the central tables whilst 'lesser' mortals were placed in the 'wings', the one-deck high bays to each side. One story tells of an elderly gentleman boarding *Caronia* in an American port, being placed in the wings. With his white stubble he did not look the part to be seen at the centre tables! Ordering steak and french-fries for most of his meals, his steward ensured that his requirements were met. Apparently the Head Waiter and Wine Steward did not pay him much attention. At the end of the trip the elderly gentleman gave a tip of several hundred dollars to his steward and sent a similar sum out to the cook who had prepared his meals. The Head Waiter and Wine Steward were suddenly attentive but received short shrift in lieu of an expected tip!

Being the designated First Class Restaurant, the Balmoral had two private dining rooms ('PDRs') off its aft starboard corner. One could seat sixteen at a banqueting table or could be rearranged for two tables of eight. The other small room could seat eight. These two PDRs were especially popular for small private parties during cruises – often these were 'theme parties' where guests had to wear the costume of a country recently visited. A typical request for a private party (this example is from one held in the Theatre Lounge, normally the Cabin Class Lounge) during the World Cruise 1964:

Mr and Mrs ('X') – (cabin) 'A' 73. Theatre Lounge. First Saturday 7.30pm
Cocktail party for 70 or 80 guests.
Champagne Bar to be set up – Mr 'X' will supply Champagne.
Small ordering bar for guests who do not take Champagne. (Separate).
Large Ice Model featuring Caviar, Foie Gras, Smoked Salmon.
Hot canapés including baked stuffed cabbage – requiring Beef wagons and one or two lamps etc., etc.
Reduce lighting. Orchestra arranged for dancing.
About 10 good waiters required for service – list to be available to Mr 'X'.

There was one other major public area. This contained the Gymnasium, Massage and Heat Treatment Rooms situated aft on 'D' Deck designed to get rid of those pounds accrued on sorties to the restaurants and café grill.

Right: First Class dining on the North Atlantic was in the royally-named Balmoral Restaurant which was was of a similar size to the equally royally-named Cabin Class Sandringham Restaurant situated aft. (The rooms are named after the Scottish and Norfolk homes of the British Monarch.) The two rooms became one class during cruises. Outside the aft starboard corner of the Balmoral Restaurant were two private dining rooms seating 8 and 16. *Cunard*

Left and Below: The Main Lounge as originally fitted (*left*). The portrait of H.R.H. Princess Elizabeth and H.R.H. The Duke of Edinburgh dominates the aft wall of this two-deck high room. Note the heavy boxed columns with lights mounted at their centres rising to the ceiling, the use of wood veneer on almost every surface and the striking contemporary design of the carpet. In the picture of this same room from after the major refit in Belfast in late 1965 (*below*), the heavy columns with their lights have been stripped away, much of the veneer appears to have been replaced, covered or painted over, opening up and lightening the room in tune with changing taste. Gone too is the distinctive carpet and there are new furnishings. The same grand piano sits beneath the portrait.

left: Cunard
below: courtesy of University of Liverpool Library

16

'Welcome, Child'

By 7 December 1948, RMS *Caronia*, official Number 182453, and with a gross tonnage of 34,187, was ready to leave her shipyard berth and proceed down the River Clyde to start, it was hoped, a long, safe and profitable career.

Captain Sorrell had travelled to Glasgow at the end of November. By the time that he reached the shipyard, he found that a suitcase containing his uniforms and mess kit had been stolen!

The crew had been hand-picked from the *Queen Mary*, *Queen Elizabeth*, *Aquitania*, *Britannic*, *Samaria* and other Cunard vessels and also from the Union Castle liners *Arundel Castle* and *Pretoria Castle*. The men travelled from Southampton to Glasgow via Euston on two special coaches chartered on the overnight train. On arrival the men were bussed to the shipyard. The crew transferred from shore-side billets to their accommodation on the *Caronia* after they signed the ship's Articles on 1 December.

Each day the crew would attend the ship, polishing, cleaning and taking on stores and learning their way around the vessel. Stores would be kept to a minimum for *Caronia*'s trials as full supplies of oil fuel, ballast, water and items that could be taken on at a later date would make the ship heavier for her speed trials

Captain Sorrell, always conscious of the value of publicity for his new ship, made sure that the *Caronia* was visible not only to the thousands who came to watch her progress down to Gourock but also to the press. The liner's giant funnel was floodlit and many of her portholes burned brightly as she lay alongside her jetty at the shipyard.

High winds of between 25 and 48 knots. failed to prevent her from sailing the 18 miles to the Tail o' the Bank on 7 December. Captain Sorrell and Dr. J. M. McNeil (Managing Director of John Brown) and John Rannie (Senior Manager) had no doubts on the matter but the pilot-in-charge, Captain J. Fisher, was not happy and said that he would not continue if the weather worsened.

On board also were 200 shipyard electricians, engineers, joiners, painters, plumbers and sub-contractors, some of whom would stay on the ship when trials began.

Before her trials could take place *Caronia* had to be dry-docked in Liverpool's Gladstone Dock to have the remains of the launch gear removed from her hull. Her bottom plates also had to be cleaned and painted after collecting much marine growth while she was fitted out afloat.

Below: *Caronia at anchor during one of her many cruises.*

Bill Archibald/John Maxtone-Graham Collection

Left: *Caronia* on sea trials during which she attained almost 24 knots in a light condition.   *Cunard*

The *Caronia* was in dry dock between 9 and 16 December when she sailed once again for Gourock to the Tail o' the Bank.

From Gourock, where she undertook compass and anchor trials, she proceeded to the measured mile off the Isle of Arran. She achieved almost 24 knots as she passed Ailsa Craig ('Paddy's Milestone'). She averaged a mean speed of 22.5 knots.

The gyro compass ceased to function so Captain Sorrell took the *Caronia* 150 miles out into the Atlantic, leading into a heavy westerly swell. Senior Cunard officials, naval architects, decorative architects and men from the shipyard were on board. Many suffered badly form the motion of the ship and a manager requested the captain to return to calmer waters, which he did.

Caronia returned to Gourock on 17 December where the shipyard men disembarked. The next day 415 guests boarded the liner from the Clyde steamer *Duchess of Hamilton* having been brought to Gourock from London and Liverpool by special trains.

The captain was informed that a special guest would be joining his ship the next evening and his crew smartened themselves for the occasion. At 8pm on the evening of the 18th H.R.H. The Duke of Edinburgh boarded the *Caronia* through a shell door on 'R' Deck along with his equerry, Lieutenant Michael Parker, R.N. Captain Sorrell was impressed with the way that the two honoured guests climbed the accommodation ladder. The captain then took the two men to inspect his well-turned out crew on Main Deck.

Soon the *Caronia* was steaming to Southampton at an average speed of 15.65 knots. The Duke addressed a dinner on Sunday night and also spoke to the crew. He said to both groups that he was sorry that his wife, Princess Elizabeth, could not be with them as she had just had a launching of her own! (Prince Charles had been born on 14 November). In his speech after the

dinner the Duke congratulated Cunard on building such a vessel so soon after the War and complimented the builders on their success.

He then wished "God speed and very best luck to the good ship *Caronia* and all who sail in her!" Captain Sorrell sent a signal to Princess Elizabeth:

'On behalf of the ship's company of the *Caronia* and the guests who are travelling with us from her birthplace, the Clyde, to Southampton, may it be permitted to express to your Royal Highness our respectful greetings from the ship which received her baptism at your gracious hand. This fine ship will, we are confident, prove herself fully worthy of the interest shown in her by your Royal Highness and by His Royal Highness the Duke of Edinburgh, whose presence among us today we regard as a signal honour and happiest of all auguries for the *Caronia*.'

Caronia arrived, dressed overall with flags, in Southampton Water on the morning of Monday 20 December. She progressed towards the docks amidst the sounds of greeting from other ships and headed towards Berth 107 in the Western ('New') Docks.

As she passed by the old, four-funnelled *Aquitania* in Berth 106, the veteran liner signalled 'Welcome, child'. The captain asked his officers for a suitable response, but the Duke suggested that the captain reply 'Greetings, Mother.' *Caronia* was alongside Berth 107 by 1pm. Between 20 December and 4 January 1949, the ship entertained various groups on board including a reception for the civic dignitaries of Southampton. On 3 January the Board of Trade inspected the liner. All the boats were lowered, the crew were mustered and Door and Fire Parties were chosen.

The next day the maiden voyage of the *Caronia* began against a backdrop of a grey sky. Her sailing was delayed by two-and-a-half hours as she did not pull away from her berth until 3pm on 4 January.

Dressed overall, the liner proceeded down the River Test to its confluence with the Itchen where the two

Right: The Wheelhouse. The inclinometer seldom indicated a roll during rough weather of (as Captain Sorrell said in 1949) "... more than 17°." During trials the ship somehow developed a list of 11° but this was soon rectified.
courtesy of University of Liverpool Library

Right: 11 January 1949 *Caronia* arrives in New York on her maiden voyage and is immediately dubbed the 'Green Goddess.' Parties continued for the four days she remained at her pier.   *Peter Smith Collection*

Below: A maiden voyage special edition of the *New York Herald Tribune European Edition* welcomes the ship into an austere post-war world.   *Len Thompson Collection*

Right: Captain Donald Sorrell, first Master of the *Caronia* with American passenger Mr Arthur Stair who had made the maiden voyage of the first *Caronia* in 1905.
Shipbuilding & Shipping Record

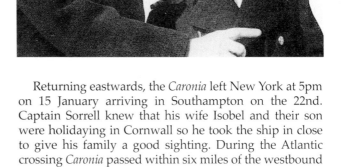

rivers create Southampton Water. As the *Caronia* passed the Ocean Dock spectators on the *Queen Mary* waved in greeting. The *Queen Mary* had returned from Cherbourg two days previously, breaking her voyage to New York after grounding on a shingle bank at Cherbourg.

Caronia, insured for £4,014,000, sailed on to Cherbourg with 200 First and 290 Cabin Class passengers, arriving at 8.30 pm. Another 190, having travelled from Paris in a special boat train, would join the ship in Cherbourg during the 3 hour stay. Even so, the ship was just over half-full.

The liner behaved perfectly in the rough seas and swells that were encountered during the course of the voyage and she arrived in New York on 11 January, docking at 8.54 am.

An American, who came aboard as the ship stopped at Quarantine before sailing up the Hudson to her dock, dubbed her immediately the 'Green Goddess'. This epithet would remain with her for the rest of her career.

In the best romantic traditions of the sea, a stowaway was discovered the day before arrival in New York. Norman Crute had boarded in Southampton with a white jacket and blue trousers in his possession. He had shared a cabin with crew members, had eaten with them in the galley, had cleaned and carried and had operated passenger lifts. Apparently, he had grown too sure of himself, had borrowed an identity card and even queued for overtime pay! Chief Master-at-Arms Beedie later found Crute hiding in the after rope locker. On landing, the stowaway was transferred to the *Queen Mary* for return to England.

Returning eastwards, the *Caronia* left New York at 5pm on 15 January arriving in Southampton on the 22nd. Captain Sorrell knew that his wife Isobel and their son were holidaying in Cornwall so he took the ship in close to give his family a good sighting. During the Atlantic crossing *Caronia* passed within six miles of the westbound *Queen Mary*. Both liners were floodlit for the occasion.

The next sailing of the 'Green Goddess' from Southampton on 29 January would include a call into Bermuda *en route* to New York. This would enable British holiday-makers to disembark and give her crew a foretaste of the sun in winter.

Captain Sorrell always kept his crews' best interests to the fore and arranged to have a swimming pool constructed out of canvas and spars on the fore deck. This was greatly appreciated and would remain a 'permanent temporary' fixture for years to come.

As the *Caronia* headed to New York she crossed over the Gulf Stream and the change from summer back to winter was almost instantaneous.

But the liner would not be away from the sunshine for long.

17

Some Cruises and Bruises!

aronia was now at the beginning of a brilliant career. On 12 February 1949 she sailed from New York to begin a season of four cruises in the Caribbean, each lasting two weeks. The itinerary on all occasions would be New York, La Guiara, Curacao, Cristobal, Kingston, Havana (in pre-Revolutionary Cuba where *Caronia* (I) pioneered Cunard's involvement with that city), and back to New York.

On completion of the cruises the ship returned to Southampton on 29 April and then spent nearly all of the remainder of the year on the North Atlantic Southampton–le Havre–New York run, completing nine round-voyages on this service.

An incident on arrival in Southampton in October had kept *Caronia* in port for seven days, two longer than usual. High winds, of up to 50 knots, during the afternoon caused the ship to over-run her berth in the New Docks and whilst she was being manoeuvred back into position the wind caught her once again, forcing her bow against the quay wall at a place where there were no fenders to protect her. Two shell plates were buckled about twenty feet above the waterline and her paint was scraped for

forty feet aft of the damaged area. It was noted that the quay wall had only suffered minor damage! The liner was inspected the following day with temporary repairs being made. Full repairs were deferred until her annual overhaul and she was able to proceed to New York.

In mid-November the 7 by 5 foot portrait of Their Royal Highnesses Princess Elizabeth and Prince Philip by Edward Halliday was hung in the Main Lounge as part of the liner's annual overhaul in Liverpool. The painting's gilded frame, specially carved by Donald Gilbert, bore the arms of the Duchess of Edinburgh.

Caronia's Atlantic sailings recommenced on 8 December and four days before Christmas she departed for the West Indies from New York adding Nassau, St. Thomas (where cheap fuel could be found), Ciudad Trujillo, Fort de France and Trinidad to her schedule.

Cunard had decided that their new vessel had the potential of being a real dollar earner and that her sphere of cruising could be profitably extended. As a result, *Caronia*'s next voyage from New York was entitled 'The Great African Cruise' with an '...itinerary to put the tang of discovery and adventure back into travel.' *Caronia* would call at twenty five ports before completing her first major cruise at Southampton. To advertise the cruise Cunard sent out luxury booklets (describing the ports of call) with covers finished in flock representing zebra skin.

Leaving New York on 12 January 1950 *Caronia* crossed the Caribbean to Trinidad then sailed down the South American eastern seaboard before calling at Baia. After this she sailed down to Rio de Janeiro for a three day visit. A dentist (a passenger) asked the captain if he could go ashore at Tristan da Cunha to study the Islanders' teeth. To enable this to happen Captain Sorrell called for extra speed and, on arrival, anchored close inshore. However, kelp was sucked into the ship's condensers and Chief Engineer Horsburgh requested that the captain take the vessel further out. Subsequently, on letting go the anchor, it was found that the *Caronia*'s bows overhung the island shelf and the anchor ran away into very deep water. It was stopped just in time to prevent it from ripping out the anchor cable stowages.

Arriving in Cape Town on 4 February 1950 for a five day stop-over, divers were sent down to inspect her hull as the *Caronia* had lost some 300 tons of fresh water during her recent passage. Leaking rivets were found to be the cause and repairs were left until the ship called at Durban. Meanwhile, many of the passengers had disembarked to experience Africa's interior on tours arranged for them by American Express and Thomas Cook. The passengers would later rejoin the ship at Mombasa where a sign was hung above the shell embarkation door proclaiming 'Welcome Home.' Officers

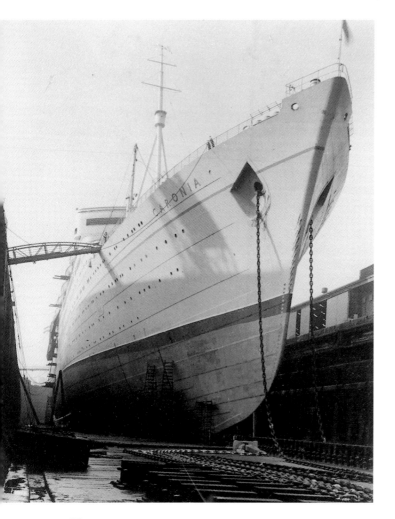

Left: As part of her annual overhaul, the *Caronia*'s anchors and cables were lowered to the floor of the Graving Dock in Liverpool for inspection.

courtesy of University of Liverpool Library

Above: *Caronia* arrives at Cape Town, with Table Mountain in the distance, on her first round Africa cruise.
Willie Farmer Collection

Left: A late 1940s, early 1950s view of the world is portrayed in this cover of the booklet for the *Caronia*'s first Great Africa Cruise in 1950.
Willie Farmer Collection

standing by a green painted lifebuoy at the base of the gangway greeted each returning passenger by name.

In those still formal days it was customary to 'dress up' rather than 'down' and, even when seated in local boats, ladies could be seen wearing smart dresses and hats and gloves!

At the time, restrictions were being lifted on imports of exotic animals into the U.K. and many of *Caronia*'s crew decided to take some parakeets home. There was a cabin on 'C' Deck forward, unoccupied on tropical cruises because hot pipes running through it made the room uninhabitable. It made an ideal home for several parakeets! If one happened to succumb, it was given a mock funeral by the crew before being dispatched over the side. A monkey, too, was purchased but because it was noisy and untrained in simple decencies, it disappeared one night, presumably throwing itself overboard.

Passengers, too, often bought unusual presents. On a later cruise Captain Thelwell recalled that one passenger was allowed to ship a rickshaw back to the U.S. but balked when another asked if he could ship a baby elephant with which his young daughter had fallen in love!

Continuing through the Suez Canal *Caronia* entered the eastern Mediterranean calling at Israel, Greece,

Right: At Mombasa, passengers rejoining the ship after travelling overland from Cape Town were greeted by officers and a 'Welcome Home' sign over the door.
Peter Jackson

Algiers (where, from his own ship HMS *Magpie*, H.R.H. the Duke of Edinburgh, Lieutenant Philip Mountbatten, boarded the *Caronia* to inspect the portrait of his wife and himself for the first time), Gibraltar, Portugal and Cherbourg before arriving home in Southampton on 26 March. Those of the original 561 passengers who had not disembarked in Europe (one American gentleman had died at Nice) or elsewhere caught one of the *Queen*s for the final leg home.

Left: Captain Donald Sorrell and the ship's staff prior to the 1950 Great African Cruise.

David Hutchings Collection

57½ years (any persons less than thirty used to organise special clubs!). The 'Goddess' was equally popular with the crew as the supply of tips was prodigious.

Having left home on 8 December *Caronia*'s 682-strong crew (extravagantly, more than one crew member per passenger) arrived home after an absence of three months ready to spend their hard earned cash. The crew loved their jobs – they could see the world *and* get paid for doing so!

Eleven return Atlantic voyages (in August she avoided a 140 knot hurricane and a 100 foot high unseasonable iceberg and, on 14 November, lost an anchor at le Havre, let go to prevent her colliding with the quay wall when a gust of wind had caught her), a refit in Liverpool and a single Caribbean cruise brought the *Caronia* into 1951, ready for an eastabout circumnavigation of the globe.

This first Round the World Cruise, covering 32,000 miles, was not fully booked. The outbreak of the Korean War the previous year had deterred many American prospective passengers. The cruise was advertised in a lavish red and gold book which revealed the delights of passing through the Panama Canal, visiting Acapulco and Los Angeles before steering towards the South Sea islands and calling at New Zealand. Australia followed, then the ship headed north to Singapore, Colombo and Bombay where the 'Goddess' stayed for eight days allowing her passengers to discover India on Thomas

The fares for this 73 day, 19,000 mile cruise had cost her American and Canadian clients between $2,400 and $12,000 and had to be paid only in U.S. dollars – the *Caronia*'s *raison d'être*. She had earned a staggering $7 million in fares and purchases! There had been twenty three millionaires on board and the average age had been

Left: *Caronia* is manoeuvred into Sydney harbour. The 'permanent temporary' swimming pool originally constructed from canvas and spars in 1949 can clearly be seen on the foredeck. On World Cruises this pool was the focus of Crossing the Line ceremonies to initiate first-time crew and passengers. The passenger's own pool was too sacrosanct to use for such a purpose.

Willie Farmer Collection

Below: Passengers on World Cruises were issued with *Caronia* luggage labels.

John Maxtone-Graham Collection

ROUND THE WORLD CRUISE
CARONIA
NAME
STATEROOM
CUNARD LINE

Right: *Caronia* steams into Wellington, New Zealand on her 1954 World Cruise.
Carola Ingall Collection

Below: Route map from the 1959 World Cruise brochure. *Cunard*

Cook's organised tours in specially provided air-conditioned trains provisioned by the ship. It was while the *Caronia* was at Bombay that passenger Sir Arthur Guiness died from heart failure on 12 March, six days after being admitted to the *Caronia*'s well-equipped hospital with kidney disease and pneumonia.

Aden, Suez, the Holy Land, Greece, Italy, Gibraltar, Lisbon, Cherbourg and home – Southampton! The crew managed some shore leave with long-separated families.

Four transatlantics were followed by a new venture – the *Caronia*'s first cruise to the Norwegian North Cape, the northernmost point in Europe. This cruise from New York to the 'Land of the Midnight Sun,' called first at Reykjavik in Iceland.

On arrival at the North Cape, and before the passengers had awoken, the crew had been busy. Volunteers had gone ashore to the Cape (in those days uninhabited except for a few guides who went home at night because of the cold) and had manually carried tables, coffee urns and provisions up the steep mountain (only rough paths and steps to walk on!) so that the passengers could have hot coffee and sandwiches on the way up and further refreshment from a champagne and brandy bar at the top. After this strenuous experience there were no more volunteers, and work details from the crew had to be organised on future visits!

After working on the mountain at midnight the stewards had to return to the ship and prepare breakfast in the restaurants.

While the *Caronia* was calling in at the spectacular Gerainger Fjord a Mrs. Donaldson died (such events

Right: From a brochure, passengers enjoy a carnival cocktail or two in the Cabin Class Cocktail Bar. This bar became the Raleigh Bar during World Cruises and attained a notoriety as being the 'watering hole' of the regular 'tipplers.' *Cunard*

were expected amongst a mostly elderly passenger list that consisted largely of the widowed, retired and the wealthy) from a cerebral haemorrhage whilst in the Raleigh Bar. This bar (the Cabin Class Cocktail Bar and Smoking Room when on the Atlantic run) would achieve a notoriety as the place in which the 'over-thirsty' would tend to congregate. One story tells of a lady who, immediately on boarding, went straight to the barman requesting that he put water into the gin bottle as her husband was over-fond of that particular spirit. The barman agreed and a tip exchanged hands. A while later the lady's husband came in and asked whether his wife had been in and had she asked the barman to put water in the gin bottle? Well, if that was the case then put gin in the water jug! Another tip was exchanged.

In the days before credit cards made sharp practices impossible, some barmen were out to make a 'quick buck.' A favourite ploy was to wait until a customer had what the barman considered to be enough and then rub a smear of gin or vodka around the rim of a glass and fill the glass with water. At least the tippler had the aroma of what was thought to be in the glass!

On leaving the North Cape, the 'Goddess' sailed southwards to the ports of Trondheim, Bergen,

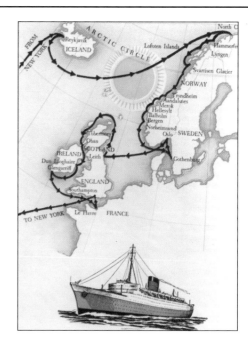

Gothenberg and Oslo before returning to the U.K. calling at Leith (the port for Edinburgh), Tobermorey, and Oban. From there it was on to the Irish Republic (Dun Laoghaire for Dublin, Glengarrif for scenery) before returning via Cherbourg for a homecoming in Southampton . At many of the calls the ship was unable to dock alongside a jetty so the 45 foot launches (which had each cost £10,000, had each been given a separate launching and were carried on the largest davits ever fitted on a ship) came into their own by ferrying passengers ashore from embarkation doors low in the shell of the ship.

Five transatlantics followed, occupying the rest of the European season. A month in Liverpool refreshed and prepared the *Caronia* for her forthcoming programme of two more transatlantics followed by a Christmas and New Year cruise to the now traditional Caribbean destinations.

Top left: *Caronia* dwarfed in the magnificent mountains of the Norwegian fjords.   *Cunard*

Top right: Brochure map showing the many ports of call on the North Cape Cruise. The route from Southamton to New York was on one of the *Queens*
Cunard/Willie Farmer Collection

Left: A campanile of Venice points skywards and the *Caronia* arrives in the Adraitic port as both crew and passengers line the rails of the 'Goddess' (sometimes alternatively known as the 'Dollar Princess.'   *Caronia Re-union*

Right: Villefranche was a port of call on *Caronia*'s first Mediterranean and European Spring Cruise in 1952.

Cunard

1952 found the 'Green Goddess' sailing from New York on her second African cruise. Following a similar route to the first a few more ports had been added including Barbados, Diego Suarez and Istanbul. Whilst transiting the Suez Canal in convoy, however, the *Caronia* went aground on 12 March. The ships ahead of her anchored in Lake Tismah whilst those behind hove to and moored along the Canal's banks. *Caronia* was aground for about an hour (because of the sensitive political situation in the area she was soon surrounded by a shoreside cordon of British troops and tanks) before she refloated under her own power.

On leaving the Canal the ship visited various Mediterranean ports before sailing home via Lisbon and Cherbourg.

Ten days were spent in Southampton before a positioning voyage took her to New York from where she began her first Mediterranean and European Spring Cruise. Her itinerary took her to Madeira; Casablanca; Cadiz; Gibraltar; Malaga; Palermo; Naples; Villefranche; Lisbon; Gothenberg; and le Havre finally reaching Southampton on 30 May.

A positioning voyage to New York followed and, after a short cruise to the West Indies, she left for her second cruise to the North Cape calling first, as before, to Reykjavik in Iceland. About two days were spent at the North Cape with passengers dancing through the night in the light of the midnight sun. Once again crew members, this time in a detailed party, had to carry provisions up the 1,500 foot mountain, wooden steps being one of the few aids. Half of the 588 passengers then made the two-and-a-half hour climb, but before they could do this they had to be declared fit.

It was while the *Caronia* was at the North Cape that a young engineering officer disappeared and two thorough searches by the Norwegian authorities failed to find him. As a result, 8th Engineer Phillip Skinner was

Below: *Caronia*'s motor launches came into their own to ferry passengers ashore where the liner herself could not get alongside, as here at Diego Suarez (now Antsiranana), Madagascar in 1964. *Caronia* had first called at Diego Suarez on her second Great African Cruise in 1952.

Bill Archibald/John Maxtone-Graham Collection

Left: Chief Engineer Willie Farmer (third from right) entertains at his table in the Balmoral Restaurant.

Willie Farmer

recorded as having 'Missed ship' in *Caronia*'s log and was owed three pounds, eight shillings and eleven pence in wages. It was thought amongst the crew that, as he 'probably' had slight communist tendencies, a Soviet submarine may have picked him up. However, this almost romantic idea came to an end a few years later when the skeletal remains of this unfortunate young officer were found. He had apparently climbed over a barrier fence, fallen down a crevasse and broken a leg.

The captain on this cruise was Captain Robert Thelwell. Other captains of the *Caronia* during her career would include Caunce; Divers; Dixon; Fasting; Fitzgerald; Grattidge; Jones (known as 'Corpus' to identify him from other Joneses in Cunard!); Law; MacKeller; MacLean; Marr; Morris; Thompson; Watts; Williams (C.S.); and Wolfenden. Captains Sorrell and Read were the first and last skippers of the 'Goddess'.

Cruising through the fjords the *Caronia* arrived in Southampton via her Swedish and Irish calls on 27 July in readiness for four transatlantic runs. A December overhaul of the 'Green Goddess' by Harland and Wolff in Liverpool's Gladstone Dock was marred by a fire in her funnel on the day before she returned to Southampton. Fifty firemen fought the blaze, which was described as a 'chimney fire'. Two firemen were hurt but otherwise no serious damage was caused.

Southampton–Bermuda–New York was followed by two of her usual Caribbean cruises. Her cruises were settling down to an annual routine. Her Caribbean excursions were aimed at those who could only afford two weeks of luxury vacation; the North Cape, Spring Mediterranean and (soon to be instigated) Autumn/Fall Mediterranean cruises appealed to those with four weeks to spare (and the money to pay for it!). The World Cruise was mainly for the very rich with both the money and the three months required at their disposal. The cabin rates, also, for the Mediterranean and World Cruises were higher than for the shorter Caribbean trips.

The operators of the excursions also settled in to a routine. Thomas Cook and Son would operate the World Cruise and 'Spring Med.'; American Express would organise the North Cape and 'Autumn Med.'

Caronia was more than fulfiling her role as a cruise ship. She was earning millions of dollars and, more importantly, she was attracting a clientele who would

travel on her again and again. Several ladies over the years would almost make the ship their homes for years on end, living ashore during overhaul periods and perhaps during the North Atlantic voyages. Clara MacBeth was one such lady.

Miss MacBeth had an apartment on Fifth Avenue, New York, but she found it cheaper to be looked after and fed on *Caronia*. Even her medical bills on board were much less than those in the States. Miss MacBeth's cabin was always A32 as the lift outside took her straight down to the Balmoral Restaurant where her usual table, a double, was just inside (forward port corner) the door nearest to the lift.

Mrs Oliver, popularly known as 'Itsy Bitsy', always booked three suites just for her luggage! Her suite was painted and varnished to her taste and she always commented if the curtains needed cleaning. She sat at the Chief Engineer's table in the restaurant and on each cruise would say, as if on her first, "I hope you don't mind me sitting on your left?" Later, when asked how many *Caronia* World Cruises she had done – "Seventeen." Her parties were legendary and her suite became known as 'Oliver's Court.' The crew even painted a special sign to say so!

Another lady always booked the same cabin, one of the cheapest, which happened to be above the noisy potato peeling machinery in the galley. Every time she travelled she complained to the Purser's office, usually to a new recruit, and each time her cabin was upgraded. One year she was 'found out' and, on booking for another cruise, was told that her cabin was unavailable as it had been turned into a stationery store!

A Mrs Jacobs always travelled with her maid, a very gentle person. Mrs Jacobs' luggage was stowed in what should have been her maid's room who was then given a 'proper' First Class cabin.

Caronia also became popular with her crew. From the officers down, a position on the 'Goddess' was known as a 'plum job,' not only because of the world travel that made a change from the routine transatlantic voyages on other Cunard ships, but because there was a chance to earn thousands of dollars in tips. It was hard work on the liner and these tips were well earned. After a long day in the hot kitchen, the staff often did not go to bed until well after 2 o'clock in the morning.

As on many ships, there was a small gay community on board *Caronia* and their exploits kept the morale going amongst the rest of the crew when it was low, especially in the tropics. The crew thought them wonderful characters. Two men known as 'Sally' and 'Lana' were especially popular. When *My Fair Lady* first appeared on Broadway 'Lana' learned all the songs and sang them in the forward 'Pig' during one of 'her' dragshows. A tall, handsome steward known as 'Marcy' used to look after the cinema theatre. One passenger, on being shown her seat, commented that 'Marcy' looked exactly like Walter Pigeon the film actor and said, "Do you mind if I call you 'Walter'?" Marcy replied, "No Madam, as long as you don't call me 'Mrs Miniver'!"

18

'There'll Always be an England!'

Caronia's luxury was becoming legendary. Her Caribbean Cruises to the West Indies and surrounding countries were always popular, not only for the beauty of the islands and the sunlit waters around them but also for the experiences of landing in exotic countries.

When she could not go alongside a pier, *Caronia* would anchor and her sixty-seat launches would ferry passengers ashore. In Willemstad, Curaçoa *Caronia* would tie up at an oiling jetty with only a ruined 'Pirates' Castle' on a distant hill as a sign of habitation. Passengers were bussed into town while the ship took on oil.

At La Guira, the port for Caracas, Venezuela, buses would again take passengers and crew into town – the ride itself was fearsome with drops of hundreds of feet alongside the rough roads!

Returning from such a cruise on the evening 4 February 1953, the *Caronia* sailed into a New York tugmen's strike. Captain Robert 'Berty' Thelwell received a message asking if he could dock his ship himself in the dark and without tugs! Docking in such conditions (luckily there was no wind, although the Hudson was running fast with snow-melt) had not been attempted before so 600 passengers and a mass of faces on land were gathered to witness the attempt. As the captain edged the 'Goddess' in towards Pier 90 an undertow caught the liner and, although 'Full Astern' was rung on the telegraphs, her bow crunched into the pier, crushing piling and masonry. Five minutes more of hectic manoeuvring and the liner was alongside the pier with no other damage than flaked paint. The passengers, nearly all American, started to sing *There'll Always be an England* as the ship made her final moves to dock!

Other large ships had also docked during the strike. The French Line's *Ile de France* had docked without incident but the *Extavia* of American Export had almost demolished a shed.

The next day the *Queen Mary* docked in an exemplary display of seamanship. Donald Sorrell, late of *Caronia*, was in command and with his 'little piece of wood' which he used to take sights, docked the liner without incident. Two of *Caronia*'s launches were sent to help take her lines ashore. The crowds that assembled to see a repeat of the spectacle that had occurred with the *Caronia*, but on a bigger scale, went away disappointed!

The *Caronia* was, happily, not delayed on sailing for her next cruise four days later. This was to be of eight weeks duration – her 'Round South America Cruise.' The route would take her though the Panama Canal, down the West Coast of South America, through the Straits of Magellan, to return via Buenos Aires and Rio de Janeiro then back to New York via the West Indies. One of the highlights of this cruise was a call into Mas A Tierra, in the Juan Fernandez Islands, famed as being the island of shipwrecked Robinson Crusoe.

The South American cruise was followed by the 'Spring Med.'; a transatlantic; the 1953 North Cape and the West Indies cruises followed by further transatlantics. The 'Autumn Med.' would be introduced in 1954.

The North Atlantic route was busy with extra traffic generated by the Coronation of Queen Elizabeth II. Of ten Cunard ships at sea on 23 March, six were U.K. bound carrying more than 6,700 passengers. The *Caronia* was the last of the fleet to arrive in Britain before the pageant, arriving in Southampton on 1 June at the end of a special Coronation Cruise. Her passengers had a bonus of reserved seats at Apsley House in London from where they could watch the Coronation procession. During those few days they could also use the *Caronia* as a hotel. For the Coronation Cruise, the passenger list had been

Above: *Caronia* took 12 feet off the head of Pier 90 when docking in New York without tugs in February 1953.
Shipbuilding & Shipping Record

bound in royal blue with a gold cord and toggle. An ice sculpture of the new Queen's head had been carved for the buffet table but unfortunately it was not long before the royal nose had started to drip!

1955 passed almost without incident other than for some steering gear trouble experienced at Malta which delayed her sailing for a day. Generally, the *Caronia* arrived and sailed from each port on time, especially during her cruises.

On her World Cruise in 1956 *Caronia* made what appears to be an unscheduled stop at Tristan da Cunha to take on fresh water. While anchored there a fishing boat crashed against her side and sank. The fishermen were picked up by the liner and a collection of £166 was raised by the passengers to replace the lost boat.

Returning to New York she sailed a few days later on

her 'Spring Med.' During this cruise the *Caronia* called in at Catania in Sicily. Here, 572 of the 744 passengers disembarked to sight-see and travelled overland to Messina in expectation of rejoining the ship there.

As *Caronia* was approaching the entrance to the port of Messina at 1.30 am on 1 June, strong currents caught her and pushed her on to a sandbank where she grounded 300 yards off-shore. She was aground for eight hours until refloated with the aid of five Italian tugs.

She then continued to Naples where an inspection revealed that, although it was thought that the keel under her bows was slightly dented, there was no other damage and her seaworthiness remained unimpaired. Captain Morris reported a few days later that divers had found nothing more serious than 50 foot of grazed paintwork. This was confirmed when the ship was dry-docked in Southampton for a more thorough inspection. Unfortunately, as she was entering the dock for this inspection a gust of wind caught her and caused a collision with the dock wall! Plates on her starboard side were damaged and temporary repairs had to be made.

1956 finished with a North Cape cruise, two transatlantics and an 'Autumn Med.'.

Arriving in Liverpool on October 16, *Caronia* was due for a major overhaul, lasting until 2 January 1957. During this period, air-conditioning would be fitted in all areas of passenger accommodation and also in the crews' quarters. On many cruises in tropical areas passengers and crew sometimes slept on the open decks (the crew keeping to the foredeck) The morning watch which had the job of hosing down the foredeck often did so with much more relish if their companions were still asleep!

During the course of the work several small fires were discovered and dealt with. Many of these were caused by contractors' men not wanting to go all the way home to return early in the morning they slept illicitly on board. Not being fully conversant with shipboard rules in dry-dock they had enjoyed a cigarette before going to sleep – or rather fell asleep whilst having a cigarette – and this was the cause of some of the fires. Sparks from a welder's torch also ignited a pile of shavings in an electrician's store on 'B' Deck. Along with false alarms,

the Bootle fire brigade was called to the ship twenty one times! Quartermaster Len Thompson remained on duty on the ship in the expanded fire-watching group. Twenty-five men continuously patrolled the ship feeling bulkheads and doors for any signs of heat and keeping a close watch for other signs of fire.

During *Caronia*'s overhaul in Liverpool from 20 November to 28 December 1958 a degaussing coil was fitted inside the hull plates and through the accommodation on 'A' Deck. The coil had been taken into the ship and fed down through the forward hatch. This multi-stranded copper cable would have a low current passed through it and would aid in de-magnetising the steel hull when sailing in areas where it was suspected that magnetic mines might have been laid. This was likely at this time in the waters around the Suez Canal. Trials of the coil took place on an Admiralty range off Weymouth in Dorset on 28/29 December, with repeated runs being made over the designated course.

Two years previously, fog had delayed the *Caronia*'s departure from Liverpool for trials. As she steamed down the Mersey an incoming tanker refused to give way to the liner which had to veer starboard. A sudden loud crunching was heard and it was thought that the ship had hit a buoy. Dining officers rushed from the restaurants and, as no internal damage was found, it was decided to carry on with the trials, but she had developed a bias in steering.

She returned to Liverpool to be dry-docked and it was found that a midship portion of bilge-keel had been torn away from the hull. The likely cause was a collision with the revetment of the Crosby Training Bank East, one of two long, underwater barrages of rubble and concrete blocks designed to scour the main channel of sand drifting in from the Crosby and Formby sands. The *Caronia* had had a lucky escape. Other ships, such as the *Lochmonar* thirty years earlier, had broken their backs on these hidden man-made banks.

The ship sailed directly from Liverpool for Bermuda, Kingston, Nassau and New York on 2 January 1957, leaving out the usual Southampton call because of the delay caused by the accident.

The *Caronia* was always difficult to steer, especially in a quartering sea, and her huge funnel often acted as a sail in strong winds, probably being the cause of many incidents in her career. Quartermaster Len Thompson attributed some of her stubborn ways to too small a rudder, saying that she always needed a 3 to 4 degree compensation at the wheel to keep her on a straight course. First Officer Peter Jackson recalls that when freshly fully loaded with fuel and water on leaving port, she was always 3 feet down at the head, which also made her "a bitch to steer!"

A combination of funnel wind resistance and steering pecularities would later conspire to create one of *Caronia*'s most bizarre accidents!

19

'A Yen to Sail'

Although 1957 would prove, as far as *Caronia* was concerned, fairly event free, romance blossomed carefully nurtured by the 'Green Goddess'.

Captain Fasting, late of the *Britannic*, had as his Junior First Officer on that ship a young Peter Jackson. Fasting was transferring to the *Caronia*, the posting for Cunard's Senior Captain, and when he asked Peter Jackson to join him as his Navigator, the young officer thought that this would place him 'above his station,' but delightedly accepted.

Because of the large number of elderly people that the *Caronia* carried, the ship required a proportionate medical team. This team comprised two doctors; three nursing sisters; a physiotherapist; one dispenser and two hospital attendants (one for night duty, one for day).

Nursing Sister Pamela Jackson (Peter, knowing that Pamela had also been on his old ship, had already noted her name above his on the Crew List) also joined *Caronia* from *Ivernia* while the liner was in overhaul in Liverpool and initially thought the 'Goddess' to be terribly scruffy. There was no water in her cabin so she had to shower in a female doctor's cabin but the liner soon became 'ship-shape.'

Pamela's job was to run the crew surgery and look after passenger requirements at night (the Senior Nursing Sister looked after the passengers by day). Duties were ten days of day-duty and then ten of nights.

The officers occasionally held parties in their wardroom to which the nurses would be invited and Pamela Jackson was duly invited to one *en route* to Bermuda. From then Peter started to see her regularly.

Four months later at Yokohama Thomas Cook and Sons gave some officers and nurses free shore excursion tickets to look after the passengers on various tours, as was usual. Pamela had gone ashore and Peter remained on board on a day off. On her return Peter 'popped the question'. The engagement party was held on a Wednesday as the *Caronia* crossed the International Date Line. With two Wednesdays – 'A' and 'B' – in which to celebrate, it must have made for a very long party!

Above: A group of officers in summer whites on the 1966 'Spring Med.' pose for the Camera. Now Senior First Officer, Peter Jackson is seated front left next to him is Staff Captain Doug Shimmon with Captain William Law third from the left.   *Peter Jackson*

Right: *Caronia* alongside South Pier in Yokohama. *Himalaya* of the P&O Line is moored at the other side of the Pier. *Port of Yokohama*

On another occasion as *Caronia* crossed the International Date Line she 'missed' one day completely. A special 'See What You Missed' programme was printed with entries such as 'Special Dance instruction by Mr Fred Astaire' etc.

The new air-conditioning plant fitted on the ship in Liverpool was working well but, in Rio, a group of crew complained that their cabins were too hot. On inspection it was found that they had the portholes open! Not even the *Caronia* could cool down South America!

Although the crew were generally happy with life on board the *Caronia* there were, as in any walk of life, tragic as well as light-hearted and comic intervals.

There were several suicides amongst the *Caronia*'s crew over the years. In September 1959, a First Class waiter, Thomas Watson, jumped overboard at a position of 30°36'N 76°10'W. Another crew member who witnessed the jump threw a life-buoy into the water and raised the alarm. The ship was turned around, a check of all departments made to identify the missing man, and the liner searched the area with a negative result.

The 'Swinging Sixties' had lost their charm for Bedroom Steward John Callan. In April, whilst at Balboa, 1966, strange noises emanated from a toilet on 'R' Deck (near to cabin R66) and blood was seen to be oozing from under the locked door. The door was forced and Callan was found slumped over a blood-filled sink, a razor by his side. The note that he left said that he had been depressed and had lost interest in everything.

Reported in the press as having fallen overboard, Stewardess Emmiline MacGregor's death on 25 April 1967 was considered by the crew to be suicide. The *Caronia* was sailing between Acapulco and Panama when, at position 13°50'N 94°30'W, a report was made at 8.43am that a pair of shoes had been found on a bollard. At 8.45 am the ship was turned to begin to search.

Captain Bill Law telephoned Chief Engineer Willie Farmer, "We've got a missing stewardess; probably over the side. We'll have to turn round – have you got enough oil?" The Chief responded, "Depends on the distance but we'll have a try."

Extra lookouts were posted until a body was seen floating face downwards, kept afloat by a pocket of air in the uniform. A boat was sent away and the body of the hapless stewardess was recovered at 11am in a position of 14°01'N 94°42W'.

The precision of the navigation was aided by the ship following the trail of its own rubbish bags which had been dumped overboard. In those days, before environmental awareness, the green-ness of the Caronia was not reflected in her method of waste disposal!

A few passengers too had problems which led them to take their own lives onboard the *Caronia*. While at Colombo during the World Cruise of 1959, Stewardess Mary Culshaw discovered the body of Mrs Vaughan Cooper Hall in bed in cabin M28. An inquest held in Colombo delivered a verdict of suicide.

In spite of the occasional tragedies, the crew lightened their lives by following many pursuits. Several were keen boxers and many a match was held on deck for an audience of both passengers and crew. Restaurants, galleys, recreation rooms, males and females, all had their darts teams. 'Buffaloes' and 'Foresters' had on-board lodges and musicians amongst the crew made life in the 'Pig and Whistle' livelier. Russ Conway would practice on the 'Pig's' piano between two and three in the morning, eventually finding a successful career in British show business. Lavish shows put on by the crew for the crew, were soon to be put on for passengers.

Rowing races between teams using the ship's emergency boats would take place in Acapulco and other ports, but perhaps the most famous entertainment of all was an annual football match held between the waiters of the Sandringham and Balmoral restaurants.

The matches were first held in Singapore during the World Cruise of 1955 when the Sandringham Dynamos beat the Balmoral Rangers 2-1. Held in Naples, Kobe, Haifa and Killefranch in the early years, the match eventually found a permanent home in Bergen during the 1957 North Cape Cruise, and became known as the 'Bergen Cup.' The official title was the 'Wareham and Bergen Trophies' Annual Soccer Match (Wareham after Mr Cyril Wareham, restaurant manager).

The crew dressed in different fancy-dress each year and involved the passengers in everything, even electing a pretty passenger as the Bergen Cup Queen. A procession wound its way through the Norwegian town *en-fête* for the occasion and the locals joined in with the fun.

The captain of *Caronia* became President of the Balmoral Rangers and the staff captain President of the Sandringham Dynamos and both were taken to the football stadium in horse drawn carriages. The losing team would hold a burial service in the 'Pig', a coffin bearing the name of the defeated team.

Not to be outdone, the kitchen staff developed a match with the 'Glory Hole Stewards' – the stewards who looked after the crew's accommodation. These 'Plonkies Football Matches' were played in Hong Kong with an occasional cricket match being held in Bombay.

Yokohama was a popular port of call, being close to Tokyo, adored by the crew as well as the passengers for

Left: Yet another procession in Bergen gets underway from the ship to the Wareham and Bergen Cup football match between the two restaurants. The 'Sandringham Dynamos' are about to set off. *courtesy of Keith Newman*

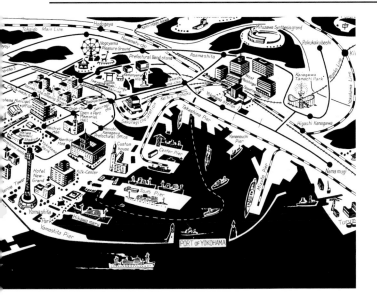

dock large enough to take her also became a problem.

On 30 April, the Japanese finally settled for a payment of ¥12,306,920 (about £12,500) to repair both breakwater and lighthouse. With Washington's approval, on 17 April, the United States Naval Forces in Japan agreed that the ship could use their dry-dock in the U.S.N. base at Yokosuka, entering the dock on 22 April.

After three days moored to her buoy, the *Caronia* was towed to the South Pier and, during a preliminary inspection, it was found that she had indeed suffered damage beneath her waterline. The damage to her stem plating had occurred between the 36 foot and 10 foot draught marks. The stem casting had been broken, part of it was missing and was replaced, temporarily it was thought, by mild steel plate.

While *Caronia* was in the U.S.N. dry-dock no one from the ship was allowed to step over a white demarcation line around the dock otherwise they were in danger of being fired at! The ship's launches, previously lowered and moored at the end of the dock, would ferry passengers and crew to and from Yokohama to enjoy the unexpected extra time in Tokyo.

shopping bargains and other delights ('Turkish bath with massage by pretty girl – one hour ¥500. Hot bath and massage all night ¥1,000!').

The Yokohama call during the 1958 World Cruise was particularly memorable as the anticipated two days extended into seventeen and some of the crew 'married' Japanese girls on six-month Shinto provisional licences!

The event that led to these blissful days began late afternoon on 14 April as *Caronia* pulled away from the South Pier and headed through the Inner Harbour towards the Outer Harbour anchorage and the open sea.

The exit between the Inner and Outer Harbours led between two breakwaters extending out from either shore and each breakwater had a lighthouse at its seaward end.

Caronia was being ushered between the lighthouses by five tugs. The two tugs ahead cast off as the 'Goddess' slipped through the entrance just as an evening gust of wind blowing down through the valleys in the mountains to the west caught *Caronia*'s huge funnel and aft structure and swung her around.

Quartermaster Len Thompson put the wheel over to port but the ship still turned to starboard. The western breakwater closed in and the *Caronia* rode over the foundation rocks, her clipper bow slicing into the breakwater until it finally touched the lighthouse, apparently an antique and historical one, which then proceeded to topple over, crashing into the sea.

Caronia backed off with 12 feet of her beautiful clipper bow twisted back to port, luckily it seemed above the waterline. The ship anchored but, fearing she would sail without paying compensation, the Japanese authorities ordered her to unshackle her anchor cable and moor against a buoy normally used for tankers. A writ was stuck to her mast.

Negotiations began on who was responsible and was going to pay. Where the *Caronia* was going to find a dry-

Top: Yokohama Harbour. The lighthouse on the breakwater (middle left) was the *Caronia*'s 'target' on her 1958 visit.   *Port of Yokohama*

Middle: The crunch! Looking over *Caronia*'s bows the crumbling masonry of the lighthouse is photographed from the foredeck.   *Len Thompson*

Below: ... the result. One antique lighthouse now defunct! *Len Thompson*

calendar's horizon.) But Honolulu was missed out as *Caronia* increased speed to make up for lost time. Speeding across the Pacific, the *Caronia* rammed and killed a whale and, to release it, had to go astern for eighteen miles. As the ship circled around the carcase and passengers took photographs, a deck hand told 9th Engineer, Harry Jupe: "This ship will never reach the breakers."

The World Cruise was followed by the 'Spring Med.' and after this a positioning trip to New York prior to the North Cape cruise. During this positioning *Caronia* hit a storm and the mast's yard arm, twenty five feet long, crashed down onto the deck. Captain Sorrell had come to the docks to see the liner sail and was taken ill shortly afterwards. His death on 25 June coincided with the fall of the spar!

Three cruises to the Caribbean ended 1958 with Havana featuring in two of them. It was while *Caronia* was in the Cuban port that gunshots were heard heralding the arrival of Revolution in the city. Passengers quickly returned to the ship and crew members were rounded up. Quite a few were just able to leave their favourite bars! As *Caronia* sailed from Havana the *Mauretania* was arriving but turned round once the sound of guns reached the ship.

Revolution was not only evident in Cuba – revolution of a different kind was in the skies. 1958 marked the year when the number of passengers travelling across the North Atlantic by air caught up with and equalled the number travelling by sea.

From this time onwards, the future of the big liners became increasingly precarious.

The dockyard workers made an excellent job of repairs but the liner's bow was never the same, always having a 'kink' in its line and seemingly making the ship even more difficult to steer.

The *Caronia* left Yokosuka on 1 May for Long Beach where many of her New York-bound passengers would disembark, due to the extra time spent in Japan.

Usually, the *Caronia* would call at Honolulu after Yokohama, a long period of nine days at sea. (Because of this extended sea-time and because it was half-way through the cruise a syndrome occurred whereby both passengers and crew began to be irritated by their companions. These days became known as 'Hate Week' but seemed to disappear as home appeared on the

Above: With a cable tying the ship to a buoy the *Caronia* remained under detention while an inquiry was instigated to assess responsibility for the damage caused to the lighthouse and breakwater.
Len Thompson

Left: *Caronia* arriving in the U.S. Naval base dry-dock to have her dented stem repaired.
Don Kent Collection

Filings and Flashes

The engines of the *Caronia* always needed special care and attention and her engineers handed down to each other the secrets of keeping the machinery operational.

The turbines had an additional nozzle called a 'By-pass'. This was intended to feed extra steam into the turbines in emergencies, such as at time of war, when an extra turn of speed might be required.

Caronia had achieved 24 knots on trials in a light condition but then her captain, Donald Sorrell, would expect 24 knots with a ship fully loaded with fuel, stores and passengers! Someone had told the captain about the By-pass nozzle, so Captain Sorrell would pass a message down 'Full speed – and open the By-pass!' which would impress people on the Bridge, but not those in the Engine Room.

Some Chief Engineers would do as requested and, as a result, the pinion connecting the turbine to the main gearing wheel would race, burring the gearing teeth on pinion and gear. Engineers would then spend time filing down the burrs on the teeth and this could only be done in port when time was available to remove the gear casing.

On one occasion the combination of high speeds and resultant burring became so bad that the gear wheel would be screaming as sufficient lubricating oil failed to reach its destination.

A new wheel, weighing 50 tons, was fitted during the long overhaul from 14 October to 30 December 1957 during the first major overhaul that *Caronia* received in Southampton.

Westbound in late September, under Captain Donald MacLean, the ship ran into the remnants of Hurricane Helene. Hailstones as 'big as pigeon eggs' thundered down as lightning flashed and heavy seas battered the ship. The radar was rendered almost ineffective as sea-clutter brought visibility down to just a few miles.

During the 'Autumn Med.' of 1959, the *Caronia* made her usual call into Istanbul and paid her first calls at the Black Sea ports of Yalta and Odessa in the then Soviet Union. Before arriving in Istanbul a wreath had been dropped in the Dardanelles during a special service of remembrance held for ANZAC soldiers who lost their lives during the Gallipoli Campaign in the First World War as many relatives were on board.

Caronia left Istanbul ready to pass through the narrows of the Bosporus into the Black Sea and a Turkish pilot had been taken on to con the ship through the busy seaway. What the pilot should have remembered was that a power line lay suspended across the channel, taking electricity from one half of Istanbul to the other. Low lying with an occasional light to illuminate its presence it hung like a waiting strand of spider's web.

Caronia's first contact came as the forward rigging of the liner took up the weight of the cable. As the ship moved forward the rigging acted like a knife as it progressively lifted the cable higher and higher. A look-out in the crow's nest filmed the event with an officer's ciné camera. Reaching breaking point, the cable parted with a loud report and a magnificent blue flash, plunging one half of Istanbul into instant darkness and cutting defence communications which set nuclear alarms ringing in NATO headquarters.

The ship's radio antenna collapsed and on shore a supporting pylon toppled over damaging several houses. Seven people were injured by the falling cable and, as 'Glory-Hole' Steward B. Cosens recalls, one of the most vociferous of the complainants was a Turk whose hapless chickens were killed!

Captain Frederic Watts filed a note of protest to the local British Consul that same day, 16 October. He stated that no notification or warning had been received from either his Turkish pilot on board nor from any other Turkish authority.

This incident somewhat detracted from *Caronia*'s good deed when in a position of 43.55N and 49.00W, on 27 September and just after 2.10 am (ship's time) she stopped to pick up a seaman, George W. Curtis, with suspected appendicitis from the American tanker *Tide*. After *Caronia*'s doctor gave the seaman a thorough medical, the liner proceeded on her way. This was just one of several errands of mercy that the 'Goddess' undertook during her career.

At the end of the 1959 overhaul in Liverpool more than 150 painters went on strike for extra pay. The liner's port side was left with rust-marks, patches of red lead and old green paint. Captain Geoffrey Marr ensured his ship was docked with her finished side landward at the ports of call during the West Indies cruise that followed. Only during an prolonged stay for the purpose in Florida when returning to New York did the ship's company finish the job, even using floodlights at night.

Captain Marr was extremely proud of his crew. In his autobiography, *The Queens and I*, he said, 'The 'Green Goddess' was a beautiful ship, a symbol of luxury and leisure, and all her days were happy days, her ship's company were beyond reproach, and were proud to sail in her as she followed the sun.'

Below: Captain Geoffrey Marr (far right) on a ship of the desert in Cairo on the 1962 'Autumn Med.'   *Geoffrey Marr*

'The Sea is Like an Ambush'
(Hugo: *Toilers of the Sea*)

As the *Caronia* sailed into the 1960s she began to show her age. Ships of more modern designs with lighter, brighter interiors were making their debuts and gradually *Caronia*'s acres of polished wood and post-war interiors started to lose their appeal.

Havana, first visited on a cruise by the first *Caronia* in 1929, had now been dropped from her annual itinerary and she now included Odessa and Yalta on the Black Sea in her 'Autumn Med.' (Her call at Yalta reflected the visit of the *Franconia* in 1945 when this Cunarder was used by Churchill when he met with Roosevelt and Stalin for a conference which partly led to the foundation of the United Nations.)

When the *Caronia* arrived in Odessa, Russian officials refused to allow the passengers to disembark unless the crew, too, could go ashore. Crew leave had been originally cancelled because the liner was experiencing bad weather and the crew was required to stand-by.

Crew recollections of their visits to Odessa include being invited for tea to find that the 'tea' was made from rose petals – real tea being too expensive for the average Russian; being followed by the KGB and seeing women labouring with shovels in the streets.

Above: King Neptune and his Court mark 'Crossing the Line' – *Caronia* style.   *Peter Jackson*

All through the life of the *Caronia* the crew managed to have fun on board and ashore; on their own or with passengers. As *Caronia* crossed the equator, the 'Crossing the Line' ceremony was a great favourite. Crew members dressed as King Neptune and his Court with first-time passengers and 'first-trippers' amongst the crew their victims. The crew's swimming pool forward was the scene of the mayhem as the passengers' pool was sacrosanct. Crossing the Arctic Circle also brought forth a similar ceremony with liberal lashings of shaving cream and foul-smelling 'gunk' being applied to the initiates.

During one World Cruise a side bet was held amongst the crew. This involved the quartermaster steering the ship in a complete circle at dead of night during the 12 to 4 watch without the officers-of-the-watch noticing. In the

vast expanses of the Pacific this could be – and was – done successfully. The captain's 'Tiger' – his personal steward – also colluded by switching off the gyro compass repeater in the 'Old Man's' quarters. Conditions had to be right – no moon, a clear night, nothing on the radar, the captain at a cocktail party and the two officers on rounds or being kept busy. At 18 to 19 knots the circle took about fifteen minutes. The money raised – and passengers often contributed – went to children's homes in Durban, Singapore, Hong Kong and San Francisco as the men who organised the illicit manoeuvre belonged to the Royal Antediluvian Order of Buffaloes, of which there were many members in all ranks on the ship. The ship's navigators were left to wonder from where the extra distances of 15 to 20 miles that were logged had appeared!

Caronia's engines again gave trouble in 1961. On 26 January, there was a failure of white metal in the No.1 (port outer) generator armature. Repairs were undertaken at Brooklyn. Five days later at Rio, the same generator shed some blades but had to wait until Cape Town before what turned out to be extensive damage could be repaired.

Cunard reported that in 1961 they had carried more passengers (177,547) across the Atlantic than any other line – although this was 30,000 below the total of 1960. The loss of some American trade was put down to the situation in Berlin.

The World Cruise of 1963 was the second that *Caronia* did sailing from east to west and it seemed to be marked by fire and water. At Bali in March the sacred volcanic mountain of Agung was erupting and *Caronia*'s sailors had to wash down her upper decks each morning to rid them of the fine ash that had settled. Luckily *Caronia* sailed before the erupting volcano did any serious damage. On the last leg of the three-month voyage the liner encountered such heavy weather off Newfoundland that a giant wave buried *Caronia*'s bows in green water and sent hundreds of tons of ocean crashing along her foredeck. The water demolished the crews' swimming pool and sent debris through windows of the Observation Lounge. Captain Marr had to duck to avoid pieces of green wreckage that flew by him on the Bridge wings.

In an attempt to bring the *Caronia* up-to-date, in 1965 Cunard decided to rebuild the vessel's afterdecks during a major overhaul. Usually, Harland and Wolff overhauled the liner at their Gladstone Dock works in Liverpool (other than for a few overhauls in Southampton) but, for such a major job, *Caronia* was sent to Harland and Wolff's Belfast shipyard.

The liner had previously called at Bangor, Co. Down, as part of her North Cape cruise but now she sailed past the town on her way to the shipyard where she arrived at 11.30 on the morning of 10 October 1965.

Here, at a peak, 1,200 men were employed on the ship undertaking the mass of work to be done. Berthed at Thompson Wharf East the ship settled down to ten weeks

Left: Sailing from Southampton on 20 August 1960 on a positioning voyage to New York from where she will undertake two West Indies cruises before sailing on the 1960 'Autumn Med.'
Southampton Daily Echo

of bustle. The re-modelling of the afterdecks centred on the construction of a new 13,000 square feet Lido Deck. This involved the removal of the old docking bridge and extending the Sun Deck. A larger, more modern, kidney-shaped swimming pool replaced the old one in a position slightly aft of the original and two new open and curved stairways gave access from the Lido to the Promenade Deck. Glazed side-screens sheltered the area.

Eight new suite rooms were also built, replacing twelve previous cabins on Main Deck. The First Class Lounge was remodelled and extended to the ship's side; alterations were made to the Observation Lounge; an extension built in the Balmoral Restaurant and a permanent cruise office was established. Kitchen alterations, launch and lifeboat renovations and usual voyage repairs were also undertaken.

A considerable amount of work was also done on the engines: turbines were stripped down and replacements made where necessary.

While at Belfast, at 6.30 am on 1 November, during a winter storm, *Caronia* broke her mooring and, as gangways crashed down onto her side, she drifted about 300 feet to the other end of the channel where she became fixed fore and aft on the bank. As soon as the tide was suitable, tugs assisted in refloating her and towed her back to her original berth where she tied up alongside at noon.

The ship was due to return to Southampton on Christmas Eve but she was ready to sail three days ahead of schedule.

The refit had cost Cunard around £500,000 although the future of shipping was still uncertain.

Right: *Caronia* again leaving Southampton, this time on 16 August 1967 near to the end of her career with Cunard. Compare the afterdecks here with those in the earlier photograph above. These decks had been extensively reconstructed during her lengthy overhaul in Belfast at the end of 1965.
Cederic J. Wasser

22

Rationalisation

Above: *Caronia* looking pristine in Southampton Docks. Painters are slung over her side giving the 'Green Goddess' a touch of make-up.   *Skyfotos*

The ageing 'Goddess' arrived back in Southampton on 23 December 1965. Four days later the fire brigade was called to the ship and panelling between the Promenade and Boat Decks had to be cut away. Electrical equipment and paint-work were damaged and firemen were at the scene for about five hours.

Caronia sailed for New York on 7 January 1966 by way of le Havre, Barbados, Kingston, Nassau and Port Everglades. During an Engineers' party (the officers on *Caronia* were encouraged to socialise with passengers – unlike on her North Atlantic counterparts) an engineer approached Chief Engineer Willie Farmer: "The ship's stopped! The fires are going out in the boilers. We must have contaminated fuel!"

"Have you changed over tanks?"

"Yes but the same thing happens."

The passengers were quietly sent away. The Chief then suggested that the boilers be fed from the settling tanks into which the contaminated fuel could be pumped to separate it from the contaminant. The fires were once again re-lit.

This arrangement lasted from Rio to Cape Town where Ricky Collinson, a ship's waiter, scuba-dived to inspect the ship's underwater hull. He found oil coming out through rivet holes and water seeping into the fuel tanks. It seemed that when the *Caronia* had been in dry-dock in Belfast, her bottom plates had been cleaned by shot-blasting with such a force that it had blown the heads off of the rivets! The subsequent inward leakage of sea water

had then contaminated the fuel. Plugs were made, and the main fuel tanks were once again rendered oil-tight.

In April 1964 Sir Basil Smallpeice had joined Cunard from B.O.A.C. as chairman and a period of severe rationalisation began. It was realised that the future of cargo transportation lay in containerisation, each container ship carrying the equivalent of several conventional cargo ships. Fast and efficient, this would change the face of world shipping forever.

For ships carrying passengers and/or cargo the future was indeed bleak. Cunard's liners started to lose money and, with increases in labour and fuel costs, for a ship like the *Caronia* which carried one crew member for each passenger, the 'writing was on the wall'.

For many British shipping companies the final blow came in the form of the Seamen's Strike of 1966. In Southampton dozens of great liners were laid up, including the *Queen Elizabeth* and *Queen Mary*, presenting a dazzling sight. The *Caronia* was caught up in this lengthy strike between June 10 and July 2. Crew from the *Queen Mary* (led by National Union of Seamen's official, John Prescott) urged the crew of the 'Goddess' to join them.

A new Cunarder, known as the 'Q4,' had been laid down at John Brown's shipyard as Yard No. 736. This vessel would ultimately be named *Queen Elizabeth 2* by Her Majesty Queen Elizabeth. Cunard required a loan to complete the vessel and, to reduce the amount of the loan, Cunard planned to sell off the less profitable as well as the older units of the fleet. *Caronia* was vulnerable.

But before the strike was over *Caronia* nearly came to a premature end. The ship's engineers were routinely emptying the condensers and, as usual, when they had emptied the water into the bilges, the *Caronia* took on a few degrees of list to starboard.

Unfortunately, the engineers did not know that portholes on 'C' Deck in the 'Pig and Whistle' were open. When the *Caronia* took on her list, water poured in through the ports flooding the compartment to a depth of eight feet.

The incident was reported in the papers as being caused by sudden blustery weather. The Southampton fire brigade was summoned to pump out the ship. Her departure on a Northern Capitals cruise was not delayed.

Having spent £500,000 on Caronia at the end of 1965. another expense lay ahead for Cunard in the *Caronia*'s next overhaul. An Act, passed in the U.S. Congress in 1966, stipulated that owners should make potential passengers embarking in the United States aware of the safety standards on their ships and that the owners should be financially able to meet any claims made against them.

To meet the Act's requirements it was planned to give *Caronia* a fire-proofing costing £100,000 during the coming overhaul.

In Rio on 11 February 1967, on what would turn out to be her last ever World Cruise, another turbo generator failed due to defective lubrication but repairs were effected by the ship's engineers.

In the first six months of 1967 *Caronia* lost £500,000. It seemed just a matter of time before an announcement concerning her future would be made.

Her final World Cruise was followed by a cruise to the North Cape which extended into the Baltic. An early 'Autumn Med.' was followed by an extra, second, late 'Autumn Med.' During the early 'Autumn Med.' the *Caronia* suffered her final injuries. At Villefranche on 13 September she encountered some very heavy weather. Her forward port mooring bitt was badly damaged and had to be removed. Her deck also required fairing and a shaft of her port anchor windlass needed to be removed, its journals machined and the bearing renewed. Five eight inch manila and two wire ropes also needed renewal. The repairs were deferred until later.

At Varna on October 19 on the late 'Autumn,' Captain 'Pip' Read and Chief Engineer Willie Farmer were invited ashore. Returning to the *Caronia* in their launch Captain Read turned to his Chief and said, "Bad news, I'm afraid. I've just opened a signal – the ship is to be sold." Mr Farmer replied, "It is bad news – for passengers and crew."

So the *Caronia* sailed to New York for the last time on 16 November. The next day she sailed for Southampton – without passengers – where she arrived at Berth 101 on 24 November 1967 to lay-up and await her fate.

Right: In Southampton on 25 November 1967, the day after her last arrival at the port, the *Caronia* still flies her paying-off pennant. The ship immediately astern of the faded 'Goddess' is the prophetically named *Caribia* (ex-*Vulcania*).

Southampton Daily Echo

23

The Last Landfall

The *Caronia* lay alongside Berth 101, the traditional lay-up berth, in Southampton's Western ('New') Docks awaiting a buyer.

A small maintenance crew remained on board to husband the ship and to display the vessel to potential buyers. Chief Engineer Willie Farmer took the opportunity to re-discover his old ship and found a memento from the first Captain of the 'Green Goddess', Donald Sorrell. On the Monkey Island atop the Wheelhouse. Captain Sorrell, a proficient artist, had left a small, personal carving in the Island's wood to mark his presence at the beginning of the liner's career.

The Cunarder's *Carinthia* of 1956 and *Sylvania* of 1957 had also been included in Cunard's restructuring programme and both ships were berthed alongside the *Caronia* also awaiting decisions on their disposal. The *Carinthia* was sold, briefly, to the Sitmar Line becoming their *Fairland* and *Sylvania*, also sold to Sitmar Line, was renamed *Fairwind*. Both would have futures as popular cruise ships, eventually coming under the aegis of P&O.

The *Caronia* remained in her solitude. In mid-January 1968 it was reported that a buyer had been found, a Yugoslavian group, Diomus-Tourist of Zagreb, had bought the liner for £1,040,000 to use as an hotel ship berthed at the medieval walled city port of Dubrovnik on the Adriatic coast.

Captain John Treasure Jones was to have command of the ship on her delivery voyage but by the end of the month the buying company had been unable to secure a permanent berth for the liner. Over the ensuing weeks the sale failed to materialise.

In March 1971 there was further speculation about *Caronia*'s future. The Swedish Government had plans to change from a two-house to a one-house parliament and the seat of government was to be re-built. While the re-building was being progressed, it was suggested, the temporarily displaced parliament staff could be cheaply housed in a passenger liner. The *Caronia* and the *Rangitane* provided choices for such a possible purchase.

However, although the £1 million proposal was under serious consideration, it was apparently regarded as 'a practical joke' by most Swedish citizens. Eventually, nothing came of the plan.

A British Conservative Member of Parliament, Mr Kenneth Lewis, suggested in the House of Commons that the *Caronia* could be used as a hostel for foreign workers in Gibraltar. This plan, too, came to nought.

Meanwhile, negotiations were underway between Cunard agents, H. E. Moss and Company, and shipbrokers Engram Shipping Company for a potential buyer. Engrams had partners including Mr A. J. Chandris , Mr R. J. Simpson and the Linnie brothers.

By the beginning of June the new owner was announced as being the Panamanian and U.S. owned Star Line. Part of the sale agreement was that the *Caronia* should not operate out of ports in the United Kingdom.

Left: *Caronia* and *Carinthia* at Berth 101 in 1968. In April complaints were received when black smoke from the 'Goddess' covered some of Southampton when she flashed her boilers to provided power for her companion.
Caronia Re-union

The group that made up the purchasing company included Mr Francis Levien of the Franchard Corporation, and Mr Andrew Konstantinides. The group stated that the ship would be employed 'exclusively in cruising' and that the liner would be brought up to the requirements of the latest maritime legislation.

In readiness for her sale the *Caronia* was dry-docked for the last time in Southampton. She was commanded for this short trip from Berth 107, to which she had been transferred, to No. 6 Dry Dock by Cunard's Captain John Treasure Jones.

Nearing retirement, Captain Jones had taken the *Queen Mary* to her retirement at Long Beach in California and had taken the second *Mauretania* (*Caronia*'s 'near-sister') to the shipbreakers in Scotland in 1965.

This would be the only time that Captain Jones would have the *Caronia* under his control. He would say years later that, because he loved the *Mauretania* and Captain 'Bil' Warwick loved the *Caronia,* they had come to a mutual agreement not to 'swap' ships, as was the custom, but to retain their own beloved commands. As a result, Captain Warwick became the only captain to take the *Caronia* ('My yacht' as he liked to describe her) on two consecutive World Cruises.

The aged *Caronia* was renamed *Colombia* in Southampton and was eventually handed over to her new owners in that port on 25 July 1968. Purchased by the Star Line for £1.25 million the representative of the new owners apparently arrived on board with cases of cash for the correct amount!

Detailed questions were asked about the *Caronia*'s engines and turbines and it was soon decided to advertise for ex-officers and engineers from the ship to help in her operation. Some young ex-Engineers applied as did an ex-Second Engineer. This latter officer became the *Colombia*'s staff Chief Engineer and would later double as cruise director and also sing as an entertainer as well as finding himself responsible for the liner's hotel services.

The *Colombia* departed Southampton on 29 July sailing for the Mediterranean and Piraeus where she was scheduled to undergo a refit.

It was hoped to have the liner ready for western hemisphere nine- and fourteen-day cruises (with prices from £117 and £200, respectively) by early December and a short, inaugural cruise to Haifa was planned. However, because of material supply problems, especially engine parts and deterioration of boiler tubes, the Haifa cruise was cancelled and her New York debut as *Colombia* deferred until February 1969.

Internally the liner underwent some changes. Many of the carpets and plush armchairs were replaced with flooring of striking patterns and contemporary wire

furniture much favoured in the late 1960s. Perhaps suitable for modern cruising, the furnishing style clashed with the polished veneers around it.

While the ship was undergoing conversion at Perama (a few miles from Piraeus where shacks served as workshops and sub-contract labour undertook the work on vessels moored stern to the land) Andrew Konstantinides bought out his partners and renamed both the ship and the owning company. She was now the *Caribia* of the Universal Cruise Line, a consortium of U.S. businessmen and a New York-based Portuguese bank.

To bring the *Caribia* up to standards compliant with current legislation and also to meet additional requirements demanded by the U.S. Coast Guard, the liner had her fire bulkheads and certain other areas sprayed with a mineral fibre compound. New fire doors to American standards (surprisingly, lower than European standards at the time) were also fitted.

Political (this was the time of the Colonels' junta in Greece) and economic (from competing Greek owners) pressures also provided seemingly insurmountable problems in getting the *Caribia* both crewed and ready for sea.

However, the ship did sail, and during the initial part of the voyage to Naples the liner suffered a fire in her funnel uptakes. This was extinguished by the Croatian Captain, the Second Engineer and by Mr Konstantinides.

The *Caribia* arrived in Naples with a crew of mixed nationalities: Greeks, Turks, Italians and a few Britons including some ex-Cunarders and, at least a 10 degree list to port. Fuel was taken on board but, because a valve was open on the opposite side of the ship, the oil went in one side and out of the other!

The *Caribia* had been painted white and her funnel gold with a narrow black capping band, but the gold paint had tarnished badly by the time the liner reached New York.

She was given a certificate for one cruise departing from New York 11 February with 500 passengers (out of a

Above: The *Caribia* arrived in Naples with a distinct list.

Right: *Caribia* remained at Naples taking on fuel before sailing for New York. *both Arthur Crook*

Left: After her disastrous Caribbean cruise, the *Caribia* languished at anchor for many months in New York harbour.
William R. Herzel

She remained at the anchorage for several months during which time she became weather beaten. An offer to buy her came in March 1970 from the Italian Lauro Line but this came to nothing.

In the Autumn the liner was berthed between Piers 84 and 86 in Manhattan. While she was there the liner was given a parking ticket but, because the authorities could not actually prove who owned the pier, Mr Konstantinides escaped prosecution and subsequently managed to pay a token rent. Access to the vessel during this period was obtained directly from the shore to the ship's stern.

During the *Caribia*'s two-year period of waiting for funds to re-introduce her to cruising there were stories of gambling parties on board held by the owner so that he could pay his crew with his winnings and of use of the vessel to make illicit films.

There were also stories about the deterioration of the liner's interiors. One relates to the New York branch of an international shipping society who met regularly on the ship. The barely heated room in which the meetings were held was lit by minimal lighting, and tales of dead rats lying in corners abounded!

Initially, the *Caribia*'s engines were turned over each week but this, too, may have ceased as the oil fuel solidified in the tanks.

Andrew Konstantinides lived aboard his ship in a suite surrounding M41, one of the old deluxe suites on Main Deck, still hopeful of his liner's return to service. By March 1971 he still needed $2 million to get the ship ready to commence a regular weekly service to Bermuda and Nassau, hopefully, in June. There was

capacity for 862 in 396 cabins). Complaints abounded on her return. Food, poor service and a foul odour that permeated the ship from a faulty waste system were listed high on the petition submitted by dissatisfied passengers.

Adjustments were made and she set off on her second cruise on 28 February with 325 passengers. Five days later, on leaving St. Thomas, a steam line ruptured in the Engine Room killing one crew member and starting a fire which destroyed the *Caribia*'s electrical systems. Out of control, the ship drifted until, 20 hours later, she was towed back into St. Thomas where her disgruntled passengers disembarked for return to the United States.

She returned, after temporary repairs, to New York where, as a ship in distress, she anchored in Gravesend Bay off Staten Island. The first *Caronia* had also anchored here after her grounding in 1905.

Left: Moored between two New York piers the *Caribia* awaits her fate. When the ship departed for the breakers a group of retired Cunard captains gathered at the end of the old Cunard Pier in New York to watch their old *Caronia* leave. Peter Jackson, by now Captain of *QE2*, was the last Cunard officer to board the *Caribia* before she sailed. He noted the sad state of the ship, especially broken glass in her corridors.
Peter Newell Collection

also a plan to base the ship in San Juan, Puerto Rico, during the winter months.

After being moved to Pier 56 and after years of idleness, these ideas had unhappily not materialised. To cut his losses (including $50,000 monthly for maintenance), Mr Konstantinides first auctioned the liner's contents. He advised his surveyor to purchase a large suitcase and to help himself to whatever he wanted. The rest of the items (furniture, fittings, etc.) were tagged and auctioned. A New York restaurant on Fifth Avenue bought many fittings which adorned this establishment for many years. Even this sale was halted by the U.S. Customs as buyers were asked to pay tax as their purchases were taken ashore.

The liner was now in a bad condition so, reluctantly, her owner decided to sell her for breaking. He managed to get a good rate (up by 400% on current prices!) for the oil fuel remaining in her (but he omitted to tell the purchaser that this was now solid!) but he could not convince his surveyor to include the built-in water ballast as part of the ship's tonnage in accounting for her scrap price!

So, on 25 April 1974, almost unnoticed and under tow by the German ocean-going tug *Hamburg*, the *Caribia* – the old *Caronia* – left New York after five years of inactivity. Sold for $3 million she was destined for the Taiwanese shipbreakers of Kaohsiung. For a tow that was scheduled to last for three months she took on a minimal crew.

The Panama Canal was successfully navigated but the tow had to enter Honolulu when the *Hamburg* developed engine trouble. 1,300 miles after leaving the Hawaiian Islands the *Caribia* developed a list that was only rectified by the intervention of the U.S. Navy.

The *Hamburg*'s engines were still proving troublesome and the tow was scheduled to call into the U.S. island of Guam, the southernmost of the Mariana Islands.

By 12 August tropical storm 'Mary' buffeted the two vessels with winds of 55 knots. Reportedly, when three miles off Apra harbour, the *Hamburg*'s generators failed and the line to the wallowing *Caribia* was cut as the tug sought refuge in the Guam port. Three crew members on the *Caribia* were lifted off by a U.S. helicopter as the liner drifted towards the harbour. It almost seemed that her giant funnel was sailing her into safety when, in the early hours of daylight on the 13 August, she veered off course and rammed herself onto the huge rocks of the harbour's breakwaters where she became helplessly stranded.

Later that afternoon the incredible force of the sea had broken the abandoned ship into three parts that, as they sank, blocked the entrance to the harbour.

The wreckage was eventually salvaged and the whole operation filmed. The sections were cut up into smaller pieces and as these were raised gave the viewer an insight into the liner's innermost secrets. Cabins, still lined with panelling, poured water back into the harbour and the veneers of rare woods reflected light, not from polish but from sea water.

Piece by piece the old liner was lifted before being shipped to the melting pots of a scrapper's furnace.

Soon, the *Caribia* had gone but she would always be remembered by those who had served and sailed on her as the fabulous 'Green Goddess'.

Below: Battered by tropical storm 'Mary' the forward part of the broken *Caribia* points towards the rocks that had brought about her sad end.
Eric Sauder

CARONIA (III)

1999

24

'British Essence'

The 'new' *Caronia* is welcomed – but she is no stranger to the Cunard fleet. Until 11 December 1999, this lovely vessel was sailing as the five-star *Vistafjord*, one of two Norwegian cruise ships brought by Cunard in 1983 from Norwegian American Cruises.

Vistafjord had been ordered on 5 December 1969 by the Norwegian America Line as the second of two very similar cruise vessels. Her slightly smaller sister ship, the *Sagafjord* was built in France in 1964–65, and both ships were built to be employed in worldwide cruising.

The *Vistafjord* was also built for occasional North Atlantic voyages. Her design, produced by Norwegian America Line's naval architects, was similar to that of the *Sagafjord* but she would be given an extra deck and would benefit from updated shipbuilding legislation.

Her passenger accommodation would be longer than that of her sister, giving the *Vistafjord* space for an additional 100 passengers.

The order for *Vistafjord* was placed with Swan Hunter Shipbuilders Ltd on the Tyne and she was effectively the last major passenger vessel to be built in England. Her keel was laid on 19 April 1971.

At the time of building, her appearance was remarkably conservative and she has retained this classic look ever since. Built at a time when ships with engines aft (and often with twin funnels) were becoming the vogue, the *Vistafjord*, with her single funnel amidships, was given a stunningly beautiful and well-balanced profile.

The Norwegians had become very conscious of building their ships with high standards of fire protection and the *Vistafjord* would benefit from the latest technology. This philosophy would greatly please the U.S. Coast Guard as the vessel would operate mainly out of American ports carrying mostly U.S. citizens. The

Top: At the time of publication three variations of a new livery for the third *Caronia* were under consideration, differing in name style and position and the inclusion (or otherwise) of the red stripe along the superstructure. This publicity picture shows *Vistafjord* as *Caronia* (III) in one of the proposed colour schemes for all Cunard vessels.

Cunard

Left: *Vistafjord* in her original Norwegian colours at Tilbury in August 1982. *B. L. Devenish-Meares*

Above: *QE2* and *Vistafjord* at the 50th Anniversary of D-Day Review in the Solent 5 June 1994. The two vessels were also at a review here on the occasion of the 150th anniversary of the Cunard Line in 1990.   *David Hutchings*

Below: Looking very handsome in her Cunard livery, the *Vistafjord* will, on renaming, make a splendid *Caronia*. Her passenger accommodation is at a similar level of comfort to that of the 'Green Goddess.'   *Cunard*

Above: Leaving her English birthplace for Oslo and a triumphant reception, the *Vistafjord* sails down the River Tyne. *Tyne & Wear Archives*

Left: Before leaving Swan Hunter, the *Vistafjord* was named at their Neptune yard. *Tyne & Wear Archives*

fire-resistant materials chosen for the interior décor created light and airy accommodation and public rooms.

Aluminium superstructures were finding favour in the late 1960s and the *Vistafjord*'s upperworks were constructed from some 600 tons of this material supplied in plate and sectional form. Her main hull was, however, of steel.

Unlike the previous two *Caronias*, the *Vistafjord*'s structure was welded throughout, with rivets only being used to join the aluminium superstructure to the hull.

The *Vistafjord* was launched without ceremony on 15 May 1972, remarkably four months ahead of schedule enabling her to be handed over to her owners almost

exactly a year later. Technical trials took place between 6 and 9 April 1973.

Before sailing to Oslo, the *Vistafjord* was christened at Swan Hunter's Neptune yard and delivered to her owners on the 17 May 1973 at Oslo during celebrations marking Norway's Independence Day. The country's popular King Olav V came on board for the occasion and the party apparently lasted for several days. Bands marched around the Upper Deck and the ship became the main attraction for the Independence Day celebrations.

With a tonnage of 24,292 gross tons (12,771 tons net), an overall length of 629.2 feet and a width of 80 feet the *Vistafjord*'s dimensions were governed by the length and width of the dry-dock that she would use in Oslo. The crew complement of 390 has remained constant in number and Norwegian in her officers

She was originally designed to carry 550 passengers. Her six passenger decks (out of a total of ten) are Sun; Promenade; Veranda(h); Upper; Main and 'A'. Over the years the Sun Deck has been extended aft to accommodate extra passenger cabins. A small decked area reserved for table tennis disappeared during this extension work.

A Sports Deck, aft on the Promenade Deck, was also dispensed with, again to make room for additional cabins. The layout of the Veranda Deck has remained much the same but a Writing Room and Library on the port side and a Card Room/Lounge on the starboard side would later become a Casino (port) and a Gift Shop and re-sited Library (starboard). Some cabins would also

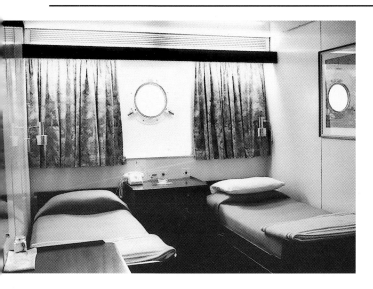

Above left: Cabin No.568 on the *Vistafjord* in 1977. Like many others it was comfortable, with twin beds, a toilet/shower and walk-in closet. All materials were fire-proofed.

Edwin Wilmshurst

Above right: The Norse Lounge on the port side of *Vistafjord* in 1977. On the refurbished *Caronia* this is now the White Star Bar.

Edwin Wilmshurst

Below: Looking forward from the Promenade Deck in 1977 were two terraced central decks.

Edwin Wilmshurst

Soon after purchase by Cunard these terraced decks were extended and joined aft to form a two-decked room that is now a night club and viewing gallery. This area is circled in the photograph (*right*) of *Vistafjord* at sea.   *Cunard*

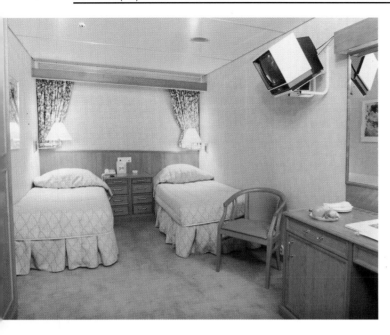

Left: An 'I' Grade inside double cabin.   *Cunard*

Saga Rose she became part of a company specialising in holidays and insurance for people over the age of 50.

Like the ships, the Cunard Line too has undergone many changes of ownership, from the British Trafalgar House to the Norwegian company Kvaerner ASA and, in 1998, into the ownership of Carnival Cruises of Miami. Carnival Cruises have achieved what J. P. Morgan's American-financed International Mercantile Marine (IMM) had failed to do in 1902 – bringing the Cunard Line in to American ownership.

A new policy of corporate identity was announced on board the *Queen Elizabeth 2* during that famous vessel's thirtieth birthday celebrations in April 1999. On this special occasion Larry Pimental, Cunard's new President and Chief Executive, announced, among other plans, a refurbishment of the *QE2* and the painting of Cunard Line's ships in a common livery of black hull (thus doing away with the dove grey hull that *Vistafjord* had worn since her launching) with white upper works topped by the distinctive Cunard red funnel. The *Vistafjord* would also be renamed under these plans. From December 1999 she would be the 'new' *Caronia*.

The *Caronia* (III) will help, as Larry Pimental stated in 'recalling the Golden Age of sea travel for those who missed the first.' Carnival's ownership of Cunard would ensure that the line would 'be the epitome of British essence, with a focus on the line's heritage.' The luxury and comfort of the five-star ex-*Vistafjord* makes her a worthy successor to her new name.

The future bodes well for Cunard – and for the *Caronia*. She is now, as Her Majesty Queen Elizabeth had said when, as Princess Elizabeth, she had launched the 'Green Goddess' in 1947, the 'heir to a great reputation.'

be enlarged during later overhauls bringing the passenger capacity up to 736. Tonnage would increase slightly to 24,492.

In 1976 the Norwegian America Line withdrew from the Atlantic service and their two remaining ships, the *Sagafjord* and *Vistafjord*, were sent on full-time cruising in mostly American waters.

In 1980 Norwegian American Cruises was formed and this company subsequently operated the two sisters until, in 1983, the vessels were acquired by Cunard. Cunard successfully marketed the *Sagafjord* and *Vistafjord* on a variety of cruises (including round the world) until the *Sagafjord* was sold in 1997. Renamed

Below: Today the ultimate in luxury at sea is represented by the Penthouse Suite. On *Caronia* (III) this is on two levels. Sleeping accommodation is on the lower level (left) with daytime accommodation above (right.).   *Cunard*

Some of the public spaces on board *Caronia* (III). The Ballroom (**above**), the Library (**top right**) and outdoor swimming pool (**right**). The interiors of the third *Caronia* are as different to those of the 'Green Goddess' as hers were to the *Caronia* of 1904. Even though of the 1970s, these interiors still retain a 'classic' appeal.   *all Cunard*

Below: *Vistafjord* at Talinin in June 1998.

B. L Devenish-Meares

Bibliography

In writing a book such as this, previously published works play an important part in its production. I am particularly indebted to the authors, editors and guardians of the following list. For further detailed reading about ports of call, passengers and the running of an ocean liner I particularly recommend the volumes by ex-captains and the works of John Maxtone-Graham to whom I am particularly indebted for his willingness to share the fruits of his own researches.

If I have unwittingly quoted without permission, future editions may, with notification, be amended with due and grateful acknowledgement and apology.

Anderson, Roy, *White Star*, (T. Stephenson & Sons Ltd., 1964)

Arnott, Captain Robert Harry, *Captain of the Queen*, (New English Library, 1982)

Bissett, Commodore Sir James, *Tramps and Ladies*, (Angus & Robertson, 1961)

Bissett, Commodore Sir James, *Commodore*, (Do)

Bobcock, F. Lawrence, *Spanning the Atlantic*, (A. Knopf, 1971)

Bonsor, N. R.P., *North Atlantic Seaway: Volume 1*, (David & Charles, 1975)

Booth, John & Coughlan, Sean, *Titanic: Signals of Disaster*, (White Star Publications, 1993)

Braynard, Frank O. and Miller, William H., *Pictorial History of the Cunard Line*, (Dover Publications, 1991)

Chesterton, E. Keble, *Steamships and Their Story*, (Cassell & Co. Ltd., 1910)

Cox, Des, *The Great Liners, Part 4: The Great Cunarders*, (Video, Snowbow Productions, 145 The Promenade, Peacehaven)

Duncan, Sylvia and Peter, *The Sea My Steed*, the Personal Story of Donald Sorrell, (Robert Hale Ltd., 1960)

Eaton, John P. and Haas, Charles A, *Titanic, A Journey Through Time*, (Patrick Stephens Ltd., 1999)

Grattidge, Captain H, *Captain of the Queens*, (Oldbourne Press, 1956)

Hurd, Archibald, *A Merchant Fleet at War*, (Cassell and Co., 1920)

Hutchings, David F., *RMS Queen Mary: 50 Years of Splendour*, (Waterfront Publications, 1986)

Hutchings, David F., *QE2: A Ship for All Seasons*, (Waterfront Publications, 1988)

Hutchings, David F., *RMS Titanic: A Modern Legend*, (Waterfront Publications, 1987)

Hyde, Francis E, *Cunard and the North Atlantic*, (MacMillan Press, 1975)

Isherwood, John, *Cunard Portraits*, (World Ship Society, 1990)

Johnson, Howard, *The Cunard Story*, (Whittet Books, 1987)

Kludas, Arnold, *Passenger Liners of the World: Vols 1 & 5*, (Patrick Stephens Ltd., 1977)

MacLean, Commodore Donald, *Queens Company*, (Hutchinson And Co., 1965)

Marr, Commodore Geoffrey, *The Queens and I*, (Adlard Coles Ltd., 1973)

Maxtone-Graham, John, *Liners To The Sun*, (Collier MacMillan, Publishers, 1985)

McCart, Neil, *Atlantic Liners of the Cunard Line*, (Patrick Stephens Ltd., 1990)

Miller, William H., *Great Luxury Liners*, (Dover Publications, 1981)

Oldham, Wilton J, The Ismay Line, (*Journal of Commerce*, 1961)

Roden, Lieut. E.C. Notes. Appointed to AMC *Caronia* August 1914 to May 1915 (unpublished)

Smallpeice, Sir Basil, *Of Comets and Queens*, (Airlife Publications Ltd., 1980)

Smith, Ken, *Turbinia*, (Newcastle Libraries and Information Service and Tyne and Wear Museums, 1996)

Thelwell, Commodore Robert G, *I Captained the Big Ships*, (Arthur Barker Ltd., 1961)

Williams, Captain G. D., *From the Captain's Table*, (Bernard Durnford, 1999)

Williams, David, *Liners In Battledress*. (Conway Maritime Press Ltd., 1989)

and also the following organisations, periodicals and newspapers for printed references:

Admiralty Library, Ministry of Defence, London

Caronia Re-union (verbal accounts and photographs)

Cunard Line (launch and travel brochures, etc.)

The Guardian, Journal of the Queen Mary Foundation (for Captain Williams' original article)

Liverpool Daily Post & Echo

Lloyds List

National Galleries and Museums on Merseyside (Documents and drawings in the Merseyside Maritime Museum)

Public Record Office (Document boxes BT100 etc.)

(Royal) Institution of Naval Architects (*Transactions*, 1914)

Sea Breezes (Steamers of the Past)

Shipping and Shipbuilding Record (S&SR)

Shipping World and Shipbuilder

Siren and Shipping

Southampton Daily Echo

Voyage, Journal of Titanic International (P.O. Box 7007, Freehold, New Jersey, USA)